THE COBRA'S DEN

THE COBRA'S DEN:

AND OTHER STORIES OF MISSIONARY WORK AMONG THE TELUGUS OF INDIA

JACOB CHAMBERLAIN

GYAN

Published by

GYAN

Gyan Publishing House
5, Ansari Road
Daryaganj, New Delhi-110002
Phone: 011-47034999, 9811692060
E-mail: books@gyanbooks.com

Distribution Network
gyanbooks.com
India, USA, Canada, UK, Australia

ISBN: 978-93-7014-233-6 (PB)

First Published, 1900

2nd Impression 2025

Printed at: Gyan Press, Delhi.

THE COBRA'S DEN

Author: JACOB CHAMBERLAIN

The Cobra's Den

THE MADANAPALLE CHURCH BIDDING FAREWELL TO DR. AND MRS. CHAMBERLAIN

The Cobra's Den

And Other Stories of Missionary Work among the Telugus of India

BY

Rev. Jacob Chamberlain, M. D., D. D.

Forty years a Missionary of the Reformed Church in America, at Madanapalle, India

Author of "In the Tiger Jungle"

TO THAT

IDEAL MISSIONARY SECRETARY

REV. HENRY NITCHIE COBB, D.D.

MY LIFELONG FRIEND

AND BROTHER

Preface

THE exceedingly kind reception given on both sides of the Atlantic, to "In the Tiger Jungle and Other Stories of Missionary Work among the Telugus" seems to indicate that such simple sketches of incidents in the life and work of any earnest, observant missionary have a place of some importance, in quickening the interest of both young people and older in all that pertains to the spread of the Kingdom, and that another collection of such sketches may not be out of place. Indeed, many urgent requests, from both friends and strangers, in Europe, Asia, and America, have been received, that at the earliest date another such collection should be issued. As these requests have come largely from acknowledged leaders in the church in the Home Lands, as well as from fellow-missionaries in different countries, and from Missionary Secretaries of many Societies and Boards, the call can no longer be left unheeded.

I have therefore made, and present herewith, another collection of sketches which have appeared in a wide variety of periodicals, in Great Britain, India and Australia, as well as in the United States, during the forty years of my missionary life. They cover a wide range of subjects, grave and gay, and illustrate very different phases of missionary life and work. They were penned, mostly, when the incidents occurred, but no attempt has been made to place them in any chronological order. Still it is believed that, in the order of thought, one leads to another. Usually each chapter is complete in itself, and the book may be opened at any point, and any sketch read independently without noticeable loss of connection.

Testimonies, received from many unimpeachable witnesses, of missionary interest quickened, or first aroused, and deeper consecration of person and purse produced by the perusal of the former volume, give stimulus to the hope and incentive to the prayer that this little volume may be used of the Master only for the arousing of His people, the promotion of His cause, and the earlier establishment of His Kingdom in the Revolted Lands of the Orient.

JACOB CHAMBERLAIN.

MADANAPALLE, India.

Contents

Introductory

"OUR Hindu Cousins" are probably the most interesting, and those most rewarding study, of any of the peoples of Asia. Whether from their ancient literature, antedating the Greek by many centuries; whether from their Primitive Religion, as set forth in their earlier Védas, contemporary with Moses and the giving of the law on Mount Sinai; whether from their ancient civilisation, dating from the time when our European ancestors were dressed in skins, roaming the forests and living in huts and in caves; whether from their country with its diversified scenery and its varied climate, reaching from the ever scorching sand plains of Cape Comorin to the forever frozen peaks of the Himalayas, where stand the tallest giant mountains of the globe; whether from their famed specimens of ancient architecture, as exemplified in the Taj and other monuments; whether from their elegant works of art, in mosaics, in carved work, in embroidery; whether from their world-famed magicians, jugglers and athletes; whether from their intricate Caste system, earliest of all Trade Unions, most effective of all Boycotts, which proved undoubtedly first a blessing to the land, and then, as it degenerated and was misused, the greatest curse resting upon them now for many generations, the people of India, in their former high estate, in their present degeneration, in the many-sided efforts now being put forth for their regeneration and uplifting, are an intensely interesting subject for study and investigation.

The story of life and work among them, on whatever lines that work may run, political, military, commercial, scientific, sociological, or religious, is sure of interested listeners if truly and realistically told. And the story of missionary life and missionary work and incident may well be known far more than it is by the Church in Home Lands, that is giving of its treasures and consecrating its sons and its daughters by increasing scores to the uplifting morally, intellectually and spiritually of India's interesting millions.

It is among the Telugu people of India that the incidents and the work depicted in the following pages have mostly taken place. The Telugus inhabit the regions from Madras northward to

Ganjam, from latitude 13° four hundred miles north to 19°, and from the seacoast of the Indian Ocean, or Bay of Bengal, west to and including large portions of the dominions of the Mahárájáh of Mysore and of the Nizam of Hyderabad.

These Telugus number nearly twenty millions of people. They, living on the seacoast, were anciently maritime in their tendencies, having, two thousand years ago, made voyages for trade and left some colonies in far off Borneo and Java and adjacent islands. They were adepts in Medicine and Surgery as long ago as Alexander the Great's invasion of India, 525 B. C., as vouched for by the historians of that invasion who speak of the aid received by them from the Ándhra (Telugu) surgeons in the treatment of their wounded. They had an extensive literature and some large libraries, which were, however, as far as possible, destroyed and obliterated by the Mohammedans when they conquered the Telugus, and sought thus to break their spirit and compass their lasting subjugation.

The Telugus are physically the tallest and best developed of all the races of Southern India and are, in the main, a courteous, kindly, intelligent, ingenuous, and now again progressive people. Their features are more of a European cast and their color from that of a mulatto to that of a Spaniard.

Of the forty distinct languages, and the one hundred divergent dialects spoken in India, the Telugu is spoken by more people than any other language with the exception of perhaps five or six. It is a mellifluous and beautiful language, possessing a very copious vocabulary, with such abundant verbal forms, conjugations and declensions, and modes, active, passive and middle, with reflexive, causative, intensive variations of all three, that it takes over one thousand forms thoroughly to conjugate and decline one such verb. It is thus peculiarly adapted to the expression of all possible phases of an idea. It is a language of Poetry and Song. Even their ancient works on grammar and arithmetic, astronomy, astrology, medicine, law and philosophy are all written in poetry, and are always chanted or intoned in reading. Their language antedates the coming down into India of the Aryans, who brought with them their still more cultivated Sanskrit, and who farther enriched the Telugu by contributing to it nearly as many Sanskrit words as the English received from the Latin and Greek languages combined. In fact about one-third of the vocables now in use among the Telugus are

Sanskrit, introduced, in their true Sanskrit form, but usually with Telugu case terminations added, into the body of the language.

The religion of the Telugus, as of all modern Hindus, is a debased form of the ancient Védic Hinduism, and is fully described in the chapter "Hinduism as it is."

It is among these Telugus that it has been my delight to live, and for them to labor for these forty years, and for whom, God willing, my remaining days are to be spent, and "My heart's desire and prayer to God for them is that they may be saved."

I

THE COBRA'S DEN

It was a hot Sunday morning in India, without a cloud in the brazen skies. We had just come home from early morning service in our Telugu Native Church, and had taken our seats at the breakfast-table. At the open door of our dining-room our Telugu school-teacher appeared and said:

"Sir, a big cobra has just been chasing a frog through the whole length of your front veranda. He struck at it again and again as it sprang past the open doors of the sitting-room, but the frog, uttering piercing shrieks,—as a frog can when pursued by a serpent,—sprang each time quick enough to elude its jaws, and together they rushed off the south end of the veranda, and the frog sprang under a box that is standing there, too near down upon the hard floor for the big cobra to get under, and so escaped."

"Where is the cobra now?"

"That is just what I don't know," said he, "for, while I was looking to see what had become of the frog, how he had got away, the cobra disappeared among the flower pots and I cannot see where he has gone."

"He must have a hole there, close by the veranda somewhere. Will you please go and watch until I come, and see if you can get sight of him again, for he must be killed, if possible, if he lives as near the house as that."

I don't go a shooting on Sunday, but I went for my pistol then, for I considered it decidedly a work of necessity and mercy to put an end to the danger of ourselves or our people being bitten by that deadly cobra. Soon appearing with a revolver, which I keep for travelling through the jungles by night, I went to hunting for the cobra's den.

Two large earthen flower pots stood about six feet from the end of the veranda, with each a beautiful rose growing in it, of which my wife was very fond, and beside which she almost daily stood picking off dead leaves, or watering and tending the roses. I soon discovered a hole in the ground about as large as my wrist, partly concealed by the grass that was growing right between the two flower pots, which were far enough apart for a person to stand between them. The hole went down perpendicularly,

SNAKE CHARMERS WITH COBRAS

THE BUNGALOW NEAR THE COBRA'S DEN

growing larger as it went deeper. It took but a moment to bring a hand mirror and throw the reflection of the bright sun right down into the hole. It revealed a horizontal chamber, or den, only a foot or so deep and the glistening scales of a cobra coiled up at rest.

Taking a piece of a broken wagon tire in my left hand to stop up the hole with, and placing the end of it slantingly in the hole, I fired down into the den. Not a motion was seen. I had missed. Turning the tire up edgewise, I fired again. What a squirming there was! His Majesty, the cobra, had been wounded. He struck up, viciously at the iron, which was turned down flat as soon as I had fired, to keep him from darting out at us. I turned the iron edgewise and fired again, and again.

When I had unloaded the sixth barrel, I let him strike his head out, and caught it against the side with the iron tire. I had brought out with me a pair of large hedge shears. With these I caught hold of his protruding neck, and with a stout pull with both hands, pulled him out and gave him a flirt out into the "compound." What a scattering there was of men, women and children! My attention had been so taken up by the snake that I had not noticed what a crowd had gathered around. Hearing the sound of shooting on Sunday in the mission compound or door-yard, they had judged that something strange was going on and had rushed in to see.

How they screamed and ran! for they did not know that the grip of the shears had dislocated the fellow's neck, and, seeing a full-sized cobra flying out toward them, they seemed to think that he was springing at them, and the soles of a good many pairs of feet were visible to one who stood near whence the snake had made his long leap.

As I had grasped the head of the cobra with the shears, I had given the wagon tire to the teacher asking him to insert the end again, instantly that I drew the cobra out, for where one cobra is you will usually find a second. I came back and threw the rays of the sun in again. Yes, there were bright cobra's scales, and another cobra wriggling.

Loading my pistol again I repeated the firing, hoping that he would strike his head up out, so that I could catch his head also. Squirm and strike as he did, his head did not come out of the hole until I had fired many times, but it finally came, and I secured him also. On drawing him out and examining him closely we found fourteen pistol ball holes through his body, and still there was fight in him. Any three of the holes would have proved fatal in time, but he died making a splendid fight. We laid the cobras out in the veranda and measured them. One of them measured five feet eleven inches, and the other six feet and two inches, than which one rarely finds a cobra larger.

Their hole showed that they had evidently been living there right among the flower pots that were tended daily and within six feet of our veranda and within twelve feet of my study door for weeks or months. A short time after some expert snake-charmers were summoned to rid our compound of serpents. In half an hour, while we were intently watching, they had, with their weird, enchanting music, charmed and enticed from holes not noted by me before, in the grass and under the shrubbery about our door yard, and dextrously captured, one by one, five more full-sized cobras. And though the cobra is the deadliest serpent known, and thousands of persons die of their bite yearly in India, no one in our mission has ever been harmed by one. Verily "He shall give His Angels charge over thee to keep thee in all thy ways" is the unbidden exclamation of many a missionary in such a time.

The above incident, as an illustration of a deep truth, has given me great cheer during the past year.

The fact is known all over Christendom that Hinduism has never been so fierce in its opposition, so vigorous and so vicious in its attacks on missionaries and their work as now. Hindu Tract Societies, Hindu Preaching Societies, have been established in the great cities, with branches all through the country. These Hindu Tract Societies issue very few books and tracts for inculcating their own religion. Nearly all of their multitudinous issues are violent attacks on Christianity and on Christ; on missionaries and their work. Every old and exploded infidel objection from the Occident is brought forth with a clang of cymbals, and made to do service in the Orient, now angrily awakening. The most absolutely untrue charges against missions, missionaries and converts, are printed and scattered by the hundred-thousand. The venom is fairly spit out in jets as was the venom of those cobras on the iron.

Hindu "preachers" are sent out from headquarters into the regions where the different missionaries are working, not to preach and explain the doctrines of Hinduism so much as to make attacks on Christianity and the missionary work. In many places their preachers seem to make little effort to gather audiences for themselves, but have messengers out here and there, and if a missionary or native pastor, or catechist gathers an audience in a street, or in a wayside shed, to tell them of the love of Christ, down they come and, taking a stand near, begin to pour out blasphemy and lies and seek to draw away or disperse their audiences.

We are not altogether sorry to have it so. Nothing is so disheartening as the stolid or contemptuous indifference so often manifested in past years. The intensity of their opposition attracts public attention widely to our message; to our weapons that are doing them this damage. We know now that Hinduism has been hit; that it has been vitally wounded. It is madly striking back in sheer desperation. My cobra friends were not disturbed by the noise of my first shots. What did they care for my banging away so long as they were not hit? But when, with better aim, the bullets began to pierce their coils, how those cobras squirmed!

Thus it is with the now intensely antagonistic

Hinduism. Sneering indifference is past. The contest waxes hot. The wild, unreasoning striking back tells of mortal wounds inflicted; presages victory for our Immanuel Captain, if we wisely, ceaselessly, zealously press the conflict. Now is the time to rally for India's conquest for Christ.

II

THE SNAKE-BITTEN HINDU'S STORY

I AM up on a little mountain in our mission district, fifteen miles from Madanapalle. It stands 1,750 feet above the Madanapalle plain, and is, in the hot season, some ten degrees cooler. I have built here a little "hermitage," to which I can come for quiet literary work. The brain works more satisfactorily and rapidly with the lower temperature and the absence of the continual interruptions to which the missionary at his own station is perpetually subject. Driving out to the foot of the mountain very early Monday morning, and climbing up the rough, crooked path to the summit soon after sunrise, I can have five clear days with my amanuensis for my work in helping to prepare Telugu Christian literature for the native Church, and go down again Friday evening to have Saturday and Sunday at my station for other duties. Thus I am up here now, but my usual isolation was interrupted one day last week by a very pleasing incident.

I was sitting at my desk writing and glancing out upon the mountain scenery when in the wide open doorway a figure appeared, and looking up I saw a man from one of our native Christian villages ten miles beyond this, who with salaams and inquiries for my health told me that he had come as the escort of a well-to-do, high-caste Telugu landholder, who lived in the caste village adjacent to theirs, and who had come up to render his thanks to me for saving his life when he was a lad and had been bitten by a deadly serpent. Would I be pleased to give him audience? He was waiting in the adjoining clump of trees to know whether I could receive him now.

He soon appeared with a tray of rock candy, cocoanuts and limes. Making low obeisance, in feeling words he expressed his gratitude to me for what I had done so long ago for him. He had sent, when I was up here the week before, saying that for fifteen years he had not had the opportunity of seeing me; might he come up here this week for the purpose? So I had had the opportunity of reviving my somewhat hazy memory of what had occurred so long ago. His name was Timmaya Reddi. His age now about forty.

"THE HERMITAGE" WHERE THE SNAKE-BITTEN HINDU TOLD HIS STORY

I asked him to be seated, and for well on to half an hour he talked, pouring out his gratitude, and recounting in minute detail the occurrences of that momentous day in his life. I have since conversed with one of our native Christians who was there and saw him after he was bitten, and saw the venomous reptile that inflicted the wound, and was at my tent while I was treating him, and who confirmed his statements in every particular. I will give his story and, where I can, will give it in his own words, turned into English.

"It was more than two decades ago—I know not just how many years—but I was then only a boy of fifteen, and now I have a wife and children. It was just after you had placed the sole of your foot down solidly at Timmareddipalle and Nalcheruvupalle, and the people of those hamlets had joined your Véda. (It must have been in the autumn of 1872 or spring of 1873, twenty-four years ago.) It was early morning. I had gone with my uncle out to our sugar-cane field to see that the irrigation channels were open and the field being properly watered. One channel seemed clogged. I pressed in among the tall cane to see what was the matter. What seemed like a reddish-brown stick of wood, larger than my arm at the shoulder, lay across the channel in the water. Leaves and grass had lodged upon it and hindered the water's flow. It was too dark for me to see that it was a sleeping serpent. I raised my crooked axe, or bill-hook, and struck it a blow to break it and draw it out of the way. The rotten log, as I thought it, squirmed and turned upon me. I saw the head, the eyes, the fangs of a deadly serpent.

"Back I sprang with all my might, shouting for my uncle. The serpent was spryer than I. Into my right ankle he drove those fangs. Ugh! How his eyes glared as he turned and ran off, showing the big gash I had made with my axe in his body, only a cubit from his head. That glare of his eyes, those horrid fangs, that blood-spurting gash in his body were the last things these eyes saw that morning as I fell over among the sugar-cane. How the pains shot up my leg! How my heart began to flutter! How soon my eyes became dim and shut as in death!

"My uncle sprang in and caught me by the shoulders just in time to see the serpent, five cubits long, disappear among the thick cane. No, it was not a cobra. Cobras are not so large; but this is regarded as equally deadly and is as much dreaded by us. Out my uncle dragged me into the open, threw me on his shoulder, ran with me to our house in the village and laid me, limp as dead, on the bench at my mother's door. I knew nothing from the time I fell over in the cane, but I have heard my uncle and my mother and my cousins so often recount all that happened that day, that I can see it all with my eyes, though they then were closed and dead, and I can tell you everything that took place that day.

"Up went the death wail. The village was gathered at our door to see me as I lay on the settee, just barely breathing. 'Do this,' said one. 'It's no use, the death mark is on him,' was the reply. 'Do that,' said another. 'Did we not try it when this very serpent bit Rámayya, and he never opened his eyes?' 'Who has a snake-stone? They say it will extract the poison. Is there not one in this village?' 'No, and if there were, one has never been known to cure the bite of this king of poisons.'

"Just then there came running up some of your Christians, who had heard the shouts and seen the commotion from their hamlet a few rods away. 'The missionary doctor! The missionary doctor!' shouted they. 'Quick! take the boy to him. He came last night to Timmareddipalle. He is in his tent there now. He never fails to cure any snake bite that is brought to him. Take him and run!'

"'Where is there a cart to put him in?' 'Don't wait for any cart. He will be dead before you can get him there by the cart road. Take him on your shoulders and run by the short cut. It's only a mile by the short footpath.'

"Onto his strong shoulders my uncle instantly threw me. Down the sloping rock, across the gully, up through the bushes on the other side and over ploughed fields he ran. Two vigorous cousins ran at his sides, and every now and then took me from his shoulder onto theirs as they ran. Down through the dry tank bed, up over the rocks, on they sped, for death was at their heels. Another cousin, the fleetest runner of the village, ran on ahead to your tent to bear the news and let you get ready. Panting, they brought me up to your tent and laid me on the grass under a tree at your tent door. You were there ready, and one of your trained men to help you, for from before sunrise your tent had been surrounded by patients whom you were treating. All gave way as they brought the snake-bitten boy up.

"'Can he cure him? Can he cure him?' ran

the question through the crowd. 'No, it is too late. He's dead already,' was the sad reply. My uncle says he thought so, too, but that you said 'Steady! no noise, no commotion, no wailing, only do as I say.' How eagerly he and they watched you.

"As they laid me down you had in your hand a bottle of that Magic Poison Killing Liquid. [Liquor Ammoniæ Fortissimus, which we use for cobra, viper and scorpion stings.] Up my nostrils you threw some of its spray; with a stick you pried open my set teeth, and poured some of it, mixed with water, into my mouth; strongly you rubbed the front of my neck and milked it down my throat. Your assistant the while was pulling open the fang wounds on my ankle with his finger nail and dropping in drop by drop the poison killer, that it might follow up the very course taken by the poison, while another was with the same magic liquid bathing the leg over the ascending vein, which was beginning to feel hard and ropy all the way up to the body.

"The commotion had all ceased. In intense expectancy the fifty people around watched all that you did, so quietly and yet so confidently. You had my arms constantly moved back and forth, also, to help the breathing, you said, and that gave my uncle something to do and made him less anxious. Half an hour had not passed before I opened my eyes and asked where I was, and what had happened, for until then you had been constantly repeating the doses of the magic fluid. Soon I sat up, and the power of the poison was gone. What wonderful medicine that poison-killing liquid is, if one knows how to use it.

"In an hour, leaning on the arm of my uncle, I walked to the house of my great aunt in the village adjacent to which your tent was pitched. Several times that day and in the evening and the next morning you came to her house to see how I got on and to administer anything further that was needed, and on the second day I walked back to my village and into my mother's house, whence I had been carried almost a corpse.

"That was before you went away to the far-off America land the first time. I saw you once after your return, at the close of the great famine, and gave you my thanks; but now for fifteen years and more I have not beheld your face. I am alive through your kindness and skill. My wife and my children revere your name and invoke blessings on your head. Five months ago I heard of your return from America once more, to this land that owes you so much, and ever since I have desired to see you, and once more tell you how grateful I am for what you did for me. I have come this ten miles on foot through the hills to-day once more to see your face and receive your benediction."

Is it any wonder that I was moved by the recital, and by his deep and reverential gratitude? My heart yearned toward him with an intense desire to do him still more good. I told him of the "Old Serpent" and of the sting of sin; of the Great Physician who can, who surely will cure all who will apply to Him; all who have that sin-venom coursing in their veins. I told him how we are all spiritually dead from this poison; how the eyes of our understanding are already closed from its venom. I told him of the blood of Jesus, that poison killer that kills the sin-venom and gives life—yes, eternal life—to every one who accepts its application and by faith clasps the hand of that Jesus Christ as his personal Saviour. I pressed him with earnest words to come to that Jesus Christ now and receive a healing far more marvellous, far more blessed than that which, by God's help, I had conferred on him. He went away thoughtful and grateful. The fruitage of this interview—may it be to him eternal life.

III

THE ANGRY MOB AND THE STORY OF THE CROSS

"SWING shut the city gates; run and tell the sentinels to stand guard and let no one pass in or out till we have made way with these preachers of other gods. No news shall ever go out of the city as to what has become of them."

It was in a walled city of some 20,000 inhabitants in the Kingdom of Hyderabad, within twenty miles of its capital, as we were on a gospel preaching tour, the first ever made through the Kingdom of the Nizam, in August, 1863, which is more fully spoken of in "In The Tiger Jungle."

We had been travelling since early morning, preaching in all the towns and villages on our way, and arrived before the gates of the city during the heat of the day, and camped outside of its walls. We had heard of it as the wickedest city of the realm.

About three P. M., my four native assistants went into the city to offer Scriptures and tracts for sale, I promising to join them when the heat should be a little less. After half or three-quarters of an hour I went through the iron gates, the largest and strongest city gates that I had up to that time seen. The city, with its high granite walls lay four square, with a gate in the middle of each side, and the main streets running from gate to gate, crossing each other at right angles at the market-place.

Just after entering the gate, I met my native assistants returning, with a hooting rabble following them. Speaking to me in the Tamil language, not understood by those people, they told me that it was not safe to attempt to do any work within the city. They had sold a few gospels and tracts to both Mohammedans and Hindus. The Mohammedan zealots and Brahman priests had been diligently examining the gospels and saw that their systems must go if these Scriptures were believed, and Mohammedans and Hindus joined in an effort to stop the people buying and drive the catechists out of the city. Herod and Pilot became friends for this purpose.

Some of the gospels were bound in yellowish buff bookbinder's muslin. The Mohammedans sent messengers running through the streets saying that they were bound in hog skin, and warning the faithful not to touch them. The Brahmans sent messengers to tell the Hindus that they were bound in calf skin, the skin of the sacred cow, and telling them not to be polluted by them. They had not only prevented the people from buying but had incited the rabble to drive the catechists out of the city.

"Have you preached to the people?" said I to the catechists. "Have you proclaimed the gospel message?"

"No, sir, we have only sold a few books and tracts."

"Then we must do so now. Did we not, before we left our home, make a solemn vow that we would not pass a single town or village without proclaiming the Master's message, and have we not His covenant, 'Lo, I am with you'? I at least must go to the market-place and preach. You need not accompany me unless you think it best."

"We did make that vow. We will go with you," said they.

The rabble had halted and quieted as they heard the foreigner talking with the catechists in a strange tongue, waiting to see what would come of it. We walked with slow and firm step up the street to the market. The crowd followed, increasing by the way. Seeing a foreigner with the catechists boldly walking up the street, the Brahman and Mohammedan zealots joined the throng.

We reached the centre of the town where the main streets crossed and where was the market-place, with a roof supported upon large masonry pillars. Stepping up the steps I said in Tamil to the catechists, "Place your backs against these pillars, so that no one can attack you from behind, and keep a sharp watch on all, but show no signs of fear. The Master is with us; His promise is good."

As we stood there we could see three of the four city gates standing wide open with the armed gate-keepers sitting under the arch of the gateways. Turning I spoke politely to the people in Telugu, which was understood by all.

"Leave this place at once," was the angry response.

I complimented them on the polite reception which they gave to visitors, telling them I had visited more than a thousand towns in the Telugu country, but that it had been reserved for them to show the most polite reception that I had thus far received. A few smiled, but the rest only scowled the more.

"Friends," said I, "I have come from far to

tell you some good news. I will tell that to you and then we will go."

"No," said some who were evidently leaders, "we will not hear you. We have found out that you have come to proclaim another God. You do so at your peril. You see this angry mob. One word from us and you are dead. Say not another word but leave the city instantly and we will see you safely out of the gates. Dare to say a word against our gods and we loose this mob on you."

We had seen the angry mob tearing up the cobble paving-stones and gathering them in the skirts of their garments to stone us with.

"We have no desire to abuse your gods," said I, "but have come to deliver a message. We will not go until we have proclaimed that message."

Then came the order, "Swing shut the gates."

I saw one nudge another saying, "You throw the first stone and I will throw the second." But all who had stones to throw were within my vision, and they quailed a little under my keen glance, and hesitated. I seemed to feel the presence of the Master as though He were standing by my side with His hand on my shoulder, saying, "I am with you. I will tell you what to say." I was not conscious of any anxiety about my personal safety. My whole soul was wrapped up in the thought "How shall I get my Master's offer of salvation before these people?"

"Brothers," said I, "it is not to revile your gods that I have come this long way; far from it. I have come to you with a royal message from a king far higher than your Nizam; I have come to tell a story sweeter than mortal ear has ever heard. But it is evident that this multitude does not wish to hear it." They thought that I was weakening and quieted down to see what was going to happen.

"But," said I, "I see five men before me who do wish to hear my story. Will you all please step back a little? I will tell these five who want to know why I have come here and what is my message, and then you may stone me. I will make no resistance then." I had been carefully scanning the crowd and had selected my men, for I had seen five honest countenances who had shown no sympathy with the abuse that had been heaped upon us.

"Brother with the red-bordered turban," said I, addressing a venerable Brahman who stood among the people at the right; "you would like to hear what my wonderful story is, before they stone me, would you not? Be frank and say so, for there are four others like you who wish to hear."

"Yes, sir, I would like to hear what your story is," said he, speaking up courageously and kindly.

"Brother with the gold-bordered turban at my left, you too would like to hear, and you with the yellow turban, and you with the brown-bordered, and you with the pink."

I had rightly judged those men, for each assented. They were curious to know what I had to say.

"Now will you five men please come forward, and I will tell you alone. All you others step back; step back; as soon as I have told these five the story you may come forward and throw your stones."

The five came forward; the rest reluctantly stepped back a little. I had purposely chosen Brahmans as I thought that I could win them the better.

"Brothers," said I, in a subdued tone, "what is it that you chant as you go to the river for your daily ablutions? Is it not this,

"'Pápóham, pápakarmáham, pápátma, pápa sambhavaha,
Tráhi mám, Krupayá Déva, Sharaná gata vatsala,'"

said I, chanting it in Sanskrit, "and is not this its meaning," said I in Telugu.

"I am a sinner, my actions are sinful. My soul is sinful. All that pertains to me is polluted with sin. Do Thou, O God, that hast mercy on those who seek Thy refuge, do Thou take away my sin."

These five Brahmans at once became my friends. One who correctly chants their Védas and their *mantras* they always look up to with respect.

"Now, do you know *how* God can do what you ask? How He can take away the burden of our sin, and give us relief?"

"No, sir, we do not know. Would that we knew."

"I know; I have learned the secret; shall I tell you?"

"Yes, sir, please tell us."

The multitude seeing the Brahmans conversing with the foreigner with evident respect, quieted still more and pressed forward to listen.

"Step back, step back," said I. "It is only these five to whom I am to tell my story. If the rest of you listen it is on your own responsibility. Step back, and let me tell these five alone." This only increased their desire to hear, as I went on:

"Brothers, is it possible for us by our own acts to expiate our sins? Can we, by painful journeys to the holiest of all your holy places, change those sinful natures that you bemoan? Does not your own Telugu Poet, Vémana say:

"The Muslim who to Tirupati goes, on pilgrimage,
Does not thereby become a saint of Siva's house.
Becomes a dog a lion when he bathes in Ganges' stream?
Benares turns not harlot into pure and trusted wife."

Hearing their own language chanted, the people pressed forward still more intently. "Nay, brothers, it is not by these outward acts even of utmost austerity that we can attain to harmony with God. Does not your beloved Vémana again say:

"'Tis not by roaming deserts wild, nor gazing at the sky;
'Tis not by bathing in the stream, nor pilgrimage to shrine;
But thine own heart must thou make pure, and then, and then alone,
Shalt thou see Him no eye hath kenned, shalt thou behold thy King."

"Now, how can our hearts be made pure, so that we may see God? I have learned the secret, and will tell you."

Then I told the story of stories; the story of redeeming love; and, as I recounted the love of

God the Father, who "so loved the world"; the birth in the manger of Bethlehem of the Lord of Life when He took on human form; His wonderful life here below; His blessed words; His marvellous deeds of healing and mercy, the mob became an audience. Gradually and imperceptibly I had raised my voice until, as I spoke in the clear and resonant Telugu, all down those three streets the multitude could hear, and as I told them of His rejection by those He had come to save, and pictured that scene on Calvary, in the graphic words that He Himself gave me that day, when for us men, and for our salvation, He was left to cry, "My God, My God, why hast Thou forsaken Me?" and told them that it was for them too, far away here in India, that He had suffered this agony on the cross, and shed His life-blood and died, down many a cheek of those who had been clamouring for our life, I saw tears coursing and dropping upon the pavements that they had torn up to stone us with. Far earlier in the story I had seen them stealthily dropping their armfuls of stones into the gutter, and come back to listen.

How they listened as I went on to tell them of the laying of His body in the tomb; of His bursting the bands of death, on the morning of the third day, and coming forth triumphing over the last enemy; of His associating for many days with, and His teaching His disciples, and of His ascension from Mt. Olivet, passing up through the clouds to be with His Father and our Father, to prepare mansions for us, and told them that now all we had to do was to repent and forsake our sins, and lift up the voice of prayer to Him, for He could understand every language, and say "O, Jesus Christ, I am a sinner. I cannot get rid of my sin, but Thou canst take it away: take away my sin I pray thee, and give me a new heart, and make me Thy disciple," and that He would do all the rest, and that when our time should come to die, He would take our souls to heaven to dwell with Him in bliss eternal.

"Now," said I, folding my arms, and standing before them, "I have finished my story. You may stone me now. I will make no resistance."

"No, no," said they, "we don't want to stone you now. We did not know whose messenger you were, nor what you had come to tell us. Do those books that you have tell more about this wonderful Redeemer?"

"Yes," said I, "this is the history of His life on earth;" and taking up a gospel of Luke I read brief portions here and there, adding, "I have not told you half of His gracious words and deeds. We are going on our way in the early morning. Would you not like to buy some of these histories of the Redeemer Jesus, so that you can learn all about Him, even though we have gone our way?"

With that their wallets were produced and they purchased all we had of the gospel of Luke; taking up another gospel I explained that the same story in the main was told in this, with different words and incidents. And taking a tract I told them that these explained the gospels, and made more clear the way of life. They purchased all the gospels and tracts we had with us, and appointed a deputation of their best men to escort us to our camp, begging us to forgive them for the insults they had heaped upon us, for they knew not whose messengers we were.

Verily the story of the cross has not lost its power. It still reaches the ear and touches the heart of men of every tongue, in every clime. Happy we, if we have a part in making known, here and in all the world that Story of The Cross.

IV

THE SURGEON'S KNIFE DETHRONES A HINDU IDOL

IT was a busy day in my little dispensary-hospital in India, 150 miles inland from Madras, in a region where up to that time, for this was more than thirty years ago, no European surgery nor medical practice had been known. I had been sent there to open out missionary work in a new region, and knew of no better way of "opening out the work" and gaining the confidence and good-will, yes, and love of the people than by following the great missionary who "went about preaching the gospel of the Kingdom and healing all manner of sickness and all manner of disease among the people." My little dispensary was built of sun-dried bricks and thatched with rushes, and would hold from seventy to one hundred people, besides the space railed off for prescribing and dispensing the medicines. In the rear was a little thatched veranda, screened with "tatties," for surgical operations.

I had opened the door as the sun peeped over the horizon. It had been given out widely that

THE MAHÁSWÁMI OF NALAPÓRAPALLE

A HINDU SANYÁSI

every one who was present at the morning preaching and prayer would be treated, no matter how long it took, before my going home for breakfast, and at sunrise we would usually find twenty to fifty already waiting at the door. A catechist sat at the door, recording the name, age and residence of all who entered, giving each one a numbered ticket, on the back of which was printed a clear, succinct statement of Christian truth, of Jesus Christ the Saviour of the world. I sat at my prescribing table, receiving the patients in the order in which they had come in, diagnosing each case and prescribing the remedies. Each one thus prescribed for sat on a bench at the side with his gospel ticket in his hand, with his name, town and number recorded on it, reading the statement of salvation by Jesus Christ printed on the back of the ticket, if they could read, while my assistant was putting up his or her medicines, for among the farmer and artisan classes women as well as men came for treatment. As the medicines were prepared they were placed in a row on a shelf at my right, to be explained and given out after the religious exercises.

As soon as the room was well filled, half an hour or more after the opening, I would push aside my medicines and instruments, and taking down my Telugu Bible read from "God's Message to Mankind," and preach the gospel of the Kingdom, one day setting forth one lesson, and another a different one, but always portraying man's lost condition, and full and free salvation through Jesus Christ and Him alone. Then telling them that we would now seek the blessing of the God of all upon us all, kneeling, with my assistants reverently kneeling around me, I would pray to Our Father to bless the physician in prescribing for the sick, guide in the dispensing of the medicines and bless the medicines so as to produce a perfect cure, and that the Great Physician would appear, and cure the malady of the soul of each one present. There was always perfect quiet and reverential attention during the brief prayer. Immediately at its close the medicines that had now been prayed over would be given out to those already treated, and then the others in the room would be treated in turn and medicines given. Surgical cases would wait until the room was cleared, or if severe and requiring chloroform, be told to come in the afternoon when I would have more time. The day of which I speak, nearly 100 of these out patients had come for treatment, besides the friends who had come with them, and who also heard the gospel message.

I had nearly completed the morning's treatment. It was approaching eleven o'clock and I was anxious to get through and go home to breakfast, when I heard the well-known semi-chant of men together bearing a burden, and looking out of the rear door I saw a sick man "borne of four," hung in a blanket, tied, hammock-like, to a long bamboo which rested on the shoulders of the four bearers.

They laid him down gently upon the floor of the back veranda, saying that they had brought him two days' journey, for they had heard that the foreign doctor effected marvellous cures, and this, their friend, was beyond the skill of their doctors. With them there had come an elderly man, led by another, an uncle of the sick young man, who, they said, had recently lost his sight, and had come in hoping that the foreign doctor could restore it. The young man was in a deplorable condition. Nothing but a serious surgical operation could save him. I very much feared that it was now too late for that,—that if it were attempted he would sink under the operation. So doubtful did I feel as to the propriety of attempting it at all, that I simply prescribed a restorative for him and for his uncle, and told them to give them nourishment and let them rest until 2 P. M., when I would examine them and see what could be done. As soon as I had finished the other patients I went home to breakfast and to rest a little, and looked up carefully, in my surgical books, the operation it would be necessary to perform, and then laid the case before the Master, asking, "Will the man endure the operation? shall I perform it? or shall I decline to perform it as hopeless? Teach me, Master, what to do." I seemed to receive the assurance that, desperate as the case was, it would prove a success, and that it might introduce the gospel message into a new region.

Buoyed up by this felt assurance, I went at two o'clock and, though with some misgiving, performed the operation. He seemed at first to have sunk under it. I cried to the Master to help. He rallied and, to my great joy, improved day by day and finally recovered. The treatment of the uncle was also so blessed of God that he recovered his sight. When at last I told them that they could now return to their homes cured, they asked if they might come to my house that evening to express their thanks and say good-bye, and they would then start with the cock-crowing of the coming morning. They came to my house, and after expressing their gratitude in the most touching and truly Oriental manner, they said,

"Will the Dora please let us have copies of 'The Divine Guru's History' (the gospels) from which you have read daily in the hospital and about which you have daily preached, and some of the 'Spiritual Teaching' (a little booklet clearly explaining the way of salvation), for we want to take them home that our friends too may know the glad news?"

"Can you read?" "No." "Is there any one in your village who can read?" "No," for they were weavers and farm labourers, and it is not the custom for them to be readers.

"Of what use, then, will the books be to you?"

"O, sir, let us have the books and we will get them read to us. When the cloth merchant comes to our village to get the cloths we weave, we will put one of these little books into his hands and say, 'Here, read us this book and then we will talk business,' and when the tax gatherer comes we will say, 'Read us this book and then we will settle our taxes.' Only let us have these books and we will see that they are read to all our village people. We too want to hear the glad sound once more, for we are never going to worship our old gods again. We will only worship the Divine Guru, Yésu Krístu (Jesus Christ), who sent you here and helped you to heal us. You never could have saved us,—so desperate a condition were we in,—unless your God had helped you. Your God shall be our God from now and forever. We want all our village to know and love Him too. Please let us have the books."

The books were given them gladly, and after farther earnest instruction in the way of Jesus and prayer to Him with and for them, we bade them farewell, saying, "When this hot season is over we are coming out with our tents touring and preaching the good news to all in your region. We will then come to your village and see you and see your people. We shall hope to find you all believers in the Lord Jesus Christ."

When the touring season began, we took our tents, myself and three native preachers, and went out into the Taluk, or county, named in the register, and preached in scores of towns and hamlets, but could hear of no village or hamlet of the recorded name. We were much disappointed. We had lost track of men whom I had believed to be in earnest.

Two years and more passed by. We were again out touring, in a county or Taluk adjoining the one where these men had been recorded as living. Our tents were pitched near a village the people of which had recently renounced heathenism, and registered themselves as disciples of the Nazarene, and were under instruction. In the central market town of the region, a mile from my tent, the weekly market was that day to be held. I had in the morning treated all the many sick that had come to my dispensary tent. At two o'clock we were all of us to go to the weekly bazaar to preach to the people who came together from fifty villages to buy and sell. Before that hour, however, I was on my bed with a very severe pull of my arch enemy, the jungle fever, and could not rise. My assistants went without me.

About sunset they returned, finding me on my cot, with the fever still burning, and said, "O, sir, we have had such an interesting time, we had a succession of large and interested audiences, and at the close two men came up and asked earnestly, 'Are you the Doctor Padre's people? and is he here? He promised to come and see us, but has never come. We want him to come, for we are all of us ready to give up our idols and join his religion.'"

The grip of my fever seemed to loosen at once with this news. Springing up, I said, "Was not one of the two men a thick-set, dark complexioned young man under thirty, whose name was Rámudu? and was not the other a tall, fair complexioned man of sixty, and his name Errapa?"

"Yes, sir," said they, "you have described the men and given their names. What do you know about them?"

"Those are the men that we were trying to find more than two years ago in the Kadiri Taluk. A mistake must have been made in recording the name of their Taluk. Where is their village? We must be there by sunrise to-morrow morning."

"It is three or four miles from here, at the foot of those hills, but you are not able to go there so soon, after such fever."

"My pony can carry me. Go we must. For more than two years have we been yearning and praying for those men. No time is to be lost now."

At four o'clock the next morning we rose, had

a cup of coffee, and a prayer to the Master to make the fifth in our party, or rather to be the first, and made our way across the fields and among the rocks. As we approached the village the sun was rising, and there, under the "Council-tree" at the head of the little village street, were gathered nearly all of the men, women and children of the hamlet, for they had seen us coming in the distance, me on my pony and my assistants walking at my side. There, with beaming countenances, were my two patients, my friends of three years ago.

"We are all ready for you," said they. "Every one in the village has agreed to give up his idols, if you will put a teacher here to teach us how to follow Jesus."

We preached to eager listeners, explaining the way of God more perfectly and prayed to Jesus to come and take possession of every heart. Soon a covenant was written out in their language and signed with his cross mark by every head of a house, for himself and family, they abjuring heathenism, renouncing their idols, placing themselves under Christian instruction, promising to observe the Sabbath, and to conform to the precepts of Christ so fast as they were taught them, and we promising, in turn, to place a teacher there to instruct them all, to teach the children to read God's word for themselves, and to lead them in the Holy Way.

After another prayer of consecration I had mounted my pony to return to our tent, for the heat was coming on. My assistants had started a shorter way, where the pony could not go, as I, sitting on my pony, had been saying a few last words. Starting on, my eye was attracted to the shrine, or little village temple under the other side of the Council-tree, where I saw half a dozen stone idols, great and small, standing on a platform at the inner end of the shrine.

"What are you going to do with these idols now?" I asked, turning to the people.

"Have we not renounced them? They are nothing to us any more."

"But are you going to leave them standing there for ignorant people to worship as they pass by?"

"What do you wish us to do? Would you like to take them away? You are welcome to them. We don't want them any more."

"I would like to take one of them," said I, thinking to test the people as to their giving them up, and wishing to send one to our supporters at home, to show what these poor people had actually been worshipping, and looked to see if I could call to one of my native assistants to take one of them. No one knows the dread these people have of their idols, their gods, and though they had renounced them, I did not like to put them to so severe a test, and so suddenly, as to ask one of them himself to do physical violence to the idols on the spot, though I knew that courage would come in time. Seeing me look for one of my people, and divining my intent, Rámudu, my old patient, stepped forward and said, "Do you want one now? I'll bring out the chief Swámi (God) and give you," and going and reaching in he shook the central and largest idol loose from its masonry setting, brought it out, and, as he reached it up to me on my pony, paused a moment and, looking at it, addressed it somewhat thus, speaking in his own language:

"Well, old fellow! be off with you! We and our ancestors for a thousand years have feared and worshipped you. Now we have found a better God, and are done with you. Be off with you and a good riddance to us. Jesus is now our God and Saviour." So speaking he handed him up to me as I sat on my horse, and now that idol adds interest to a missionary museum in the home land, as he sits among the dethroned deities conquered by King Immanuel.

When, after a few months of further instruction, it was my privilege to baptise those people into the name of the Father and the Son and the Holy Ghost, I rejoiced greatly that they had, meantime, proved their faith by standing firm through the fiery trial of persecution which had burst upon them for deserting their ancient faith, and I thanked God that the surgeon's knife had proved in that case, as in others I know of, the effective instrument in dethroning some of India's so-called gods.

Out of the more than 1,000,000 towns and villages in India, in, perhaps, 250,000 of them, through the agency of the surgeon's knife, the physician's prescription, the little village school established for adherents' children, the mission high school, the Christian college, the schools for Hindu girls, the Zenana workers, the Bible women, the colporteurs and the Christian preachers, from the missionary and native pastor to the catechist and reader, has the salvation of Jesus the Christ been made known, though as yet accepted in comparatively few of them.

But for the 750,000 towns and villages in which

no evangelistic work is going on, where rests the responsibility? Where rests the responsibility for China and for all heathendom? Where, but on that Church of God in Christian lands to whom was given the express order, "Go ye into all the world and preach the gospel to every creature." Where, but on you, O individual Christian, on whom the obligation lies to go or send? Each dollar that you give now may save a soul. Each $100 may plant the gospel in one more village.

For thine own salvation "How much owest thou thy Lord?" Take thy bill and write quickly, and then to the extent of thine ability, if not of thy debt, join hands with Him, the Great Missionary, who left His home land for this heathen world,—who saved thee,—join hands with Him, thy Prince Immanuel, in prosecuting that work which He came to inaugurate—the salvation of the whole world. Fill the treasury of thy Church's Board; send thy sons; send thy daughters, and in the Christians' home wear thou not the starless crown.

V

YES OR NO? INSTRUCTIONS WANTED

By the last mail I received an intimation that some persons in our home Church are not altogether pleased when news comes of accessions in our mission fields, for the reason that it costs to sustain the enlarged work. Some four months ago it was my privilege to send home news that several villages, or hamlets, in the region of Madanapalle had cast off their idols, renounced their false gods, and placed themselves under Christian instruction.

Several schoolhouse-chapels were at once erected, costing as much as fifty dollars apiece. Some additional readers and teachers were employed, drawing a salary of as much as four dollars and a half a month each, that the children might be taught by day, and the adults be gathered each evening and each Sunday, and instructed in the way of the Lord more perfectly; and certain prudent heads were shaken, so I infer from what I have heard, by prudent people, who did not know whether our Church was prepared to receive such an increase to her work and her responsibilities.

Now I am in a quandary. Who will tell me what I am to do? To-day I have received a written application from the inhabitants of four hamlets in another direction to be taken under Christian instruction. They promise to pitch their idols overboard; to cease working on the Sabbath; to give up everything hostile to Christianity; to live according to its holy precepts, so far as in them lies, and beg me to send some one to tell them what those precepts are. Shall I do it, or shall I not?

They are poor. So were those who came over five months ago, but they have most of them stood firm and have grown in grace. They have been abused; have been threatened; their work has been interfered with; four of them in different villages have been assaulted and beaten, one of them so that it was feared for some hours that he would not survive, simply because they refused to abjure their faith in their new-found Saviour. And, on top of it all, these four hamlets ask me to take them under instruction and receive them to the fellowship of such abuse.

What answer shall I give them? Consider well before advising me; for it will cost money. It may interfere with the erection of a $100,000 church in New York for me to spend fifty dollars in erecting a church for these inquirers in these new villages. It may interfere with the endowment of a $60,000 professorship at home if I spend seven dollars a month in supporting a catechist to show these seeking ones the way to heaven. It may complicate the arrangement for a $400 trip to the Yosemite Valley, or a $200 trip to the White Mountains, or a $1,000 trip to Europe next summer, if I ask one of the city merchants to increase his subscription by five dollars per month to support a school, in order that the children may be suffered to come unto Jesus. So would it not be better, on the whole, for me to tell this deputation that the Home Church cannot afford to have any more of them become Christians?

There was a time, I believe, when the Church really wished to establish and sustain missions in India and China and Japan. Is she frightened now that the child begins to grow? And does she wish to starve her Eastern children to death, because, forsooth, it will take so much milk to rear them up to manhood? Does she wish to gain the credit of having missions in three great empires of the East, without bearing the burden of their support?

God forbid; and yet the voice that speaks to

us month by month, through the columns of "Receipts for the Board of Foreign Missions," would almost lead a disinterested observer to form such a conclusion, and the retrenchments and curtailments that we on the ground have been compelled to make year by year leave us little spirit to rebut the charge.

We go on with our itinerating; we preach the gospel of glad-tidings in the highways and byways. When those to whom we have preached come forward and say: "Sir, we are convinced of the truth of what you say; please receive us under instruction and train us for your heaven," shall we say, "Hold on, don't be too fast. The Home Church can't afford to have you believe quite so soon"?

Little does the church at home know the burden she is, and has been, putting on her missionaries by her attitude of the past few years. We wish now to know what we are to do. Shall we gather in the fruit of what we sow, or shall we not? Shall we receive under instruction those who apply, or shall we tell them to go back to their idols and feed on ashes until the Home Church feels better able to enlarge its work? We want, through the column of Receipts for the Foreign Board, an explicit answer—Yes or No.

VI

THOSE TORN-UP GOSPELS

VÁYALPÁD is the Taluk town of the Taluk, or county town of the county, of Vâyalpâd, in India, 160 miles northwest of Madras. It is a town of not more than 6,000 or 7,000 inhabitants, but has been rather a wealthy place for its size, having a good many goldsmiths plying their profitable trade. There is also a noted Hindu temple with a large number of Brahman priests attached; and more than forty villages, within a radius of four miles, cluster around it as a centre. It is thus a place of importance in that region. What its people do, the surrounding villagers are likely to follow.

In July, 1865, three of us missionaries went there on a gospel-preaching and Bible-distributing tour. Two years before I had gone up into that Telugu country, and established a new station at Madanapalle, the Taluk town of the adjoining Taluk, and with my native assistants had been busy, in preaching the gospel and introducing the Scriptures, as far as possible, in its multitudinous villages. But now, anxious to carry the gospel into the adjacent Taluk, I had asked two other missionaries of our mission, with several native assistants to join me, that we might make a strong impression upon the people to whom we were bringing the gospel news for the first time.

We pitched our tents in a grove just out of the town, which was built compactly, with houses joining one another, as in the crowded streets of a large city.

The next morning at sunrise we went into the chief street to preach. The streets were neatly swept from house-wall to house-wall, for there are no sidewalks in their not over-broad streets. In front of each door the street was sprinkled with cow-dung water, which they use for purification, and white ornamental figures had been made on the ground, by the women of the household allowing finely powdered lime to run through their fingers as they deftly moved their hands around, to form each her favorite design.

Little was going on in the early morning as we went into the street, but the presence of several foreigners and their companions was soon noted, and when we took our stand, and in chorus sang a gospel song to one of their old familiar native tunes, an audience soon filled the streets where we were. After reading a portion from the gospel of Luke in the Telugu language, one of the native preachers first addressed the audience, and one of us missionaries followed setting forth Jesus of Nazareth, of whom we had read in the gospel, as the Saviour of all men, of every land, of every language, of every race, if they will only believe on Him, and accept His salvation as a free gift. The audience listened quietly, but with evident questionings and incredulity. We offered our gospels and tracts gratuitously, but only a very few were accepted, and that with no eagerness. We bade our audience a polite farewell, and went back to our tents. That evening we went out preaching in some of the villages beyond the town, and on returning through the Bazaar street, just at dusk, we noticed bits of torn leaves of Scriptures and tracts scattered up and down the street. As we entered our tent one of my brother missionaries said to me in a wearied, somewhat dispirited tone, "What is the use of our doing this? The people here have no desire to listen. They only tear up and throw away the Scriptures and tracts that we give them. Those books we gave this morning are all wasted."

"Not so," said I, "some of the books have

been torn up, but it strikes me that only a few, and the fragments of them diligently scattered for the purpose of producing the impression that all have been destroyed. This is a part of my parish, and I am going to test this. Those torn bits will attract attention to the books. They may serve as seed corn. I shall watch."

By eight o'clock the streets were deserted, and I sent one of our men out to gather up, by moonlight, sample bits of the torn leaves in all parts of the street. He brought them in and on a careful examination we found that they were all parts of the gospel of Luke, or of a large tract, explaining the gospels. One of each had evidently been torn up, and well scattered.

Before moving our tent back into our own Taluk to carry on our touring there, we preached in thirty-seven of the villages of that group.

It was four years before I could again get around to Váyalpád. During the interval we had preached in several thousand towns and villages in other directions. In a single year myself and three native assistants had visited 1,061 different villages, all within twenty miles of Madanapalle, and now we were able to pitch our camp again in the grove not far from the great temple at Váyalpád.

I went with my native assistants into the same street to preach. The street was filled with an audience. This time they listened closely, and discussed the points at issue with zeal. At the close we offered them the same gospels and tracts, but now on sale. We declined to give away any. A number of the more intelligent part of the audience produced their wallets and purchased. They came to our tent for further conversation, and bought more Scriptures, and when, after again preaching in the surrounding villages, we moved our camp we found that we had, on this visit, sold there 253 Scriptures and tracts. "That seed corn is sprouting," I said, and I thanked God and took courage.

Where one missionary's field or parish is the size of the state of Connecticut, with a still larger population, it is impossible to traverse the whole ground often. It was now 1883. I had, meantime, visited the place repeatedly, each time receiving a more kindly welcome. The people of an adjoining hamlet of day labourers had given in their names renouncing heathenism, and repeatedly asked to be taken under Christian instruction. I had at last sent a catechist there to instruct them. His coming was the occasion of a remarkable movement among the people of Váyalpád. It reminded them of our previous visit; of the D. vine message that we had delivered to them; of the Scriptures we had distributed. It set them talking of Christianity and of the Bible, and of the effect it had upon the lives of its adherents, and their earnest talking led them to form a singular resolution. This resolution was embodied in a petition which they sent to me by a special messenger. The details of this petition and the action that followed are given in the following chapter.

VII

THE HINDU JUDGE'S OPINION OF THE BIBLE

It was in December, 1883, that I received the very singular petition referred to in the last chapter. It was signed by some of the most influential inhabitants of the Taluk town of Vâyalpád. It asked that I should receive under my care the Anglo-Telugu school of 100 pupils which they had established the previous year, to educate their sons, and organize it as a mission school, *introducing the Bible into all the classes as a Text-Book.* Not one of the petitioners was a Christian.

Much surprised at the tenor of the request, I went out there at once to meet the people, and see whether they were sincere in making the request, and whether the supporters of the school were unanimous in the matter. On my arrival a meeting of all those interested in the school was held. The request was publicly presented to me in the same terms, namely, that I would receive the school under my care and management, and would introduce the Bible as a Text-Book into each class, to be studied daily in English in the higher classes and in Telugu in the lower.

The head master of the school, a Brahman, himself educated in a mission school, explained to those of the supporters of the school who had not been present before, the advantage of having the school under the charge of a missionary, and of studying the Bible, reminding them that he spoke from experience.

He was followed by the District Munsif, or native judge of the district court, a native gentleman of excellent character and education. Though using English fluently, he spoke in Telugu, so as to be understood by all, speaking substantially as follows:

"My friends, I was not educated in a mission school, but I have many friends who were, and who studied the Bible daily in school. I have witnessed its effects upon their lives. I have read the Bible myself privately a good deal. I have come to know the pure and beautiful system of morality it inculcates. My friends, there is nothing in our Védas that can compare with it, as I well know from careful examination. Let your sons study the Bible. They need not become Christians. There is no compulsion about it. The missionaries never force any one. But if you want your sons to become noble, upright men, put this school under the charge of the missionary, and have the Bible taught in it daily. It will make your sons better men, and you will be happier parents.

"My friends, I have but one son, as you know. On him all my hopes are centred. You know I am able to send him where I please for his education. But I want him to be a noble, earnest man. I have therefore sent him to the *Madras Christian College*, to be educated, and there he studies the Bible with the missionaries every day. This tells you what *I* think of the mission schools and of the Bible. I have done."

By unanimous vote the school was put under the charge of our mission, and no lessons are studied with more fidelity than are the daily Bible lessons, under a Christian teacher. No examinations are more creditably passed than those on the Bible by those heathen boys. And now, in addition to their daily lessons, a purely voluntary Sunday-school of sixty lads and young men has been formed, who meet every Sabbath morning for the study of the deeper spiritual meaning of this word of God. God grant that they may get more good from the study of the

Book than they expected when they asked that it be given them to study.

Those torn-up gospels mentioned in the preceding chapter have indeed borne a rich fruitage, for were they not the word of Him who said, "It shall not return unto Me void, but it shall prosper in the thing whereto I sent it."

VIII

MARKETING THE BIBLE

THE missionary among the heathen who does not engage in, and foster Bible colportage is a misfit. As well sow the rice fields on the arid plains of India with no arrangements for their subsequent irrigation. Paul plants; Apollos waters; God gives the increase. If the vernacular preaching in the towns, and the villages, the highways and the byways is Paul, then colportage, which leaves the divine word in the gospel and the tract is Apollos, left to water the seed the living voice has sown, and we may depend on God's giving the increase.

We may not see it; we may never know it, but "My word shall not return unto Me void," said one who fulfills His word. Many a soul will be found in glory from those dark lands of the earth whom no missionary, whom no other Christian has ever seen, brought there by some gospel or tract, scattered by some missionary or his colporteur; seed which they in their ignorance suppose to have been choked by the thorns, but

INDIAN BUFFALOES BATHING

A HINDU STREET SCENE

which the Divine Eye has seen to produce fruit, in spite of its thorny surroundings.

Downright earnest effort on the part of a missionary in doing Bible colportage work himself, as often as other duties will at all allow, and in keeping native colporteurs vigorously at work, stimulating them by his own methods and example, will royally pay him.

What I mean can, perhaps, best be set forth by giving an illustration from my own experience.

More than thirty years ago I took a preaching and Bible distributing journey through regions up to that time never visited by a missionary, largely at the expense of the American Bible Society.

My party consisted of four native assistants and myself, all of us preachers, all of us colporteurs. We started with two cart loads of Scriptures, Bibles, New Testaments, gospels, tracts, or booklets, explaining the gospels, and setting forth clearly the way of life, in the five languages we were to encounter, each of which could be used by some of us, for we could each of us preach in two or more, but chiefly in the Telugu language, for it was through the Telugu country that most of our journey led.

We came, one day, more than 400 miles from

our starting-point, to the old capital of the ancient Telugu empire, Warangal, which was in its glory when Columbus discovered America, containing then near 1,000,000 inhabitants, the city's walls being twenty miles in circuit. About the time of Columbus the Mohammedan invaders conquered the Telugu empire, and their capital, ere long, fell into ruin, although the old iron gates of the citadel were, when I visited it, still swinging in the gateway of the massive granite walls. Within the old city circuit are now eight detached towns, and villages, of more or less importance.

We stopped there four days to preach and sell Scriptures and tracts. At sunrise each morning we took several boxes of books in a long, low-bodied open *bandy*, or cart, drawn by bullocks, and, mounting it ourselves, drove into the streets of one of those towns. Stopping in the centre of a street, and all standing up in the cart, we joined in singing a "Gospel Call," in one of the old Telugu melodies, weird and sweet, that have come down through a dozen generations. The words, in English, would read, "O, come, brothers, come and listen to the story of Jesus and His love. Come, for the dread day of death and the judgment are fast drawing nigh. Come, for Jesus is ready to take away all your sins, and give you eternal life. Come, brothers, come, and listen to the story of Jesus and His love."

An audience soon assembled. One of my assistants would read from one of the gospels, and explain it. Then I would preach, standing in the cart so as the better to be seen and heard by all the crowd, and often half a thousand people would gather round before we had done.

After presenting as clearly and forcibly as I could God's plan of salvation through Jesus Christ His own Son, who came and suffered for us, I said to them, "Brothers! We have come a long way to tell you of this Divine Redeemer. We are to go on farther shortly. We have brought with us the history of the Redeemer, the gospels, and the whole 'True Véda,' the Bible, and little books explaining this 'new way of life.' We will sell them to you for a very small price, that you may keep them to read after we have gone on; for surely you will want to know how to obtain the love, the favor, the salvation of this Jesus the Saviour, the remission of sins, the eternal life that He, and He alone can give. Here is the story of that Redeemer, written by Luke, the physician. The price is only one *dub*, (about one cent). Who will have one?"

Out come the little wallets; up are passed the *dubs*; out are passed the copies of Luke's gospel. Down from the cart spring three of the native assistants, with each a package of the gospels in his arms, and work their way through the crowd selling as they go, while we sell on the cart. After some twenty minutes I take up a tract of the size of a gospel, explaining the way of salvation. Reading a page from it and explaining it, I offer that for sale. Up come more *dubs*, and out go the tracts. Then the Bible is read from, and once more the plan of salvation is set forth, and the Bible is offered for sale for fifty *dubs*, and then the New Testament for twenty, and each of the other gospels and tracts, in turn, is read from and sold.

When all had purchased that wished to in that street, we would drive into another and repeat the process and so again until ten or eleven o'clock, when we would return to our camp and rest until four P. M. Then we would start in another village, or another part of the town. Four days of this work resulted, as my records show, in the disposal of 1,225 books, chiefly gospels and large tracts, but including nine Bibles, and six New Testaments, and we had preached the gospel to forty different audiences.

Twenty-eight years passed. There came to my house at Madanapalle a man of twenty-five or thirty years of age, of the Merchant Caste, with a singular story. He was from the suburb of Warangal in which we had sold the largest number of books. He may have been an infant at the time we were there. He may not have been born. He did not know his exact age.

His father had died when he was a child. He was brought up by his father's brother as a son. When some twenty years of age he was one day rummaging in a cupboard of his uncle's house, when he came upon an old book. It was called the *Kotta Nibandhana*, the New Testament. He asked his uncle about it.

"O, it's a book I bought many years ago."

"Well, what is it about, uncle?"

"They said, when I bought it, that it told of a new way of getting rid of sin."

"Have you read it?"

"No. After I had bought it I showed it to our family priest, and he persuaded me not to read it. You had better not read it either. Our fathers' way is good enough for me, and for you too. Put it back where you found it."

The young man put it back. But every now

and then, secretly at first, he took it out and read parts of it. He became interested. He became absorbed. He would talk with his friends about that divine *Guru, Yésu Krístu,* and wanted to know where he could learn more about him. His uncle and friends became alarmed. They would not have him embrace a new religion. They tore up and burned the New Testament. They raised a sufficient purse, and bade him go on a pilgrimage, first to Benares, and thence to the other holy places of the Hindus, to reëstablish his faith in Hinduism. For two years he had thus wandered, visiting all the most sacred places of the Hindus.

At last he came to the Holy Mountain of Tirupati, with its splendid temples on its summit, only sixty miles from my station, and worshipped there. His mind became more and more dissatisfied with the Hinduism he saw exemplified at the successive holy shrines. He asked some of the other pilgrims if they had ever heard of people who were proclaiming a divine redeemer whom they called *Yésu Krístu.* At last he found a man who said, "Yes, there are some people of that sort sixty miles west of here, at Madanapalle, who go all around the country preaching about *Yésu Krístu,* and trying to make us give up our gods, and these our holy shrines. There don't many people believe them. You keep clear of them. Our fathers' gods are good enough for us their children. Hari! Hari! Vishnu! Jaya!" (To Vishnu be the victory!)

Secretly by night he slipped away. He came to Madanapalle. For several days he stopped in a Native Rest House, while reconnoitring the ground, and making enquiries about these strange people and their teachings. Finally he fell in with one of the very men who had stood with me on the cart, and sold the Scriptures at Warangal, and with him came to me. Earnestly did he study God's Word for some weeks, under our guidance, and then asked to be baptized into the name of that *Yésu Krístu* he had so strangely learned about, and come to love and trust.

As I pronounced the Triune Name over him, in the holy ordinance I thanked God for this new evidence of the verity of His promise, "My word shall not return unto Me void."

Scores of cases of known fruitage from the scattering of the seed in the pages of the printed truth come crowding into my mind, emphasising the importance of earnestly conducted Bible colportage in missionary work, but room fails me to give them here; nor need I. One apple from a tree gives the flavor of them all. If we press on with all vigor in this blessed work, we are well assured that "in due season we shall reap, if we faint not."

IX

A MEDICO-EVANGELISTIC TOUR

THE field which I am supposed to cultivate, with Madanapalle as its headquarters, comprises the subdivision of the Cuddapah district, *i. e.*, that portion of the district which is under the jurisdiction of the sub-collector and joint magistrate, resident at Madanapalle. It comprises four Taluks or counties, being about 100 miles in length, by about fifty in breadth. My work is mostly, of course, in the Madanapalle Taluk, and the adjacent one of Váyalpád. I have also made two tours in the northeastern Taluk of Ráyachóti, but have never before worked in this northwest Taluk, Kadiri, the nearest point of which is thirty miles, and the farthest eighty miles, from Madanapalle.

Having returned to Madanapalle from a previous tour on the first of December, I started, on the morning of the fourth, with my native helpers, for a month's campaign in the Kadiri Taluk. I brought with me three large and well-filled medicine chests, which I have prepared for just this work. One contains eighty-five vials of from one-half ounce to eight ounces in size, filled with the stronger and more expensive preparations; the other two containing more bulky articles. The three together contain about 30,400 doses of medicine. I took with me, also, one of the pupil assistants from our Madanapalle dipensary, to help me in dispensing the medicines.

Thus equipped, we moved on, by short stages from Madanapalle to Kadiri, the headquarters, or county town of the Taluk. During one night's journey we had three unbridged rivers to cross, and, in one of these the cart containing the medicines was upset, falling partly in the water. It fell down the bank so heavily, that I feared great destruction amongst the medicines, but it proved that only four bottles, containing some ten or fifteen rupees' worth of medicine, were broken.

Kadiri is a large, old heathen town, with extensive temples, and hundreds of Brahman priests. We were too tired with our morning's march and work, to go out preaching the evening of the day we arrived, but sunrise the next morning found us where four streets meet in the heart of the town, with a very large crowd of curious listeners around us. This is the first time that a missionary, or a European physician, has been in this region, and they were not a little curious to know what it meant. Mounted on the platform of a temple portico, I could be seen and heard by the crowd that extended down the four streets, while I laid before them, the true and only way of salvation, through a crucified Redeemer. After preaching, I remained, for twenty minutes, to assist the catechists in selling books, and then left them to continue selling, while I returned to my tent to attend to patients. After I left, the helpers sold about 100 books.

The first day or two, the people came rather cautiously for treatment. I had intimated, in the Bazaar street, that I would treat any who would come, but they did not understand this gratuitous treatment of the sick, so they came tentatively, as it were, the first day. Three or four Brahmans, half a dozen merchants, as many artisans, and a number of farmers came dropping in during the day, but, as each applicant for treatment brought several friends with him, we had good opportunities of preaching, to group after group, all day. The next day, more came, and to-day, the third day, I have had between sixty and seventy patients, including every class from the highest to the lowest. Doubtless, the numbers will increase while I remain here. We go out regularly, morning and evening, preaching in the town and surrounding villages, but are able to continue our Evangelistic work through the day, by means of the medical attractions to draw people together.

Monday evening. Yesterday was a busy day. Instead of going out preaching in the morning, I began my medical work at sunrise, so as to get through with all important cases by nine o'clock, and be ready for morning service in my tent. There are, at present, three gentlemen in the revenue service of government, temporarily encamped with their families, near here, and two other Europeans in government employ, also in tents, near by. Among their servants and office people, there are several native Christians, and they all joined in the request, that I would give them a Telugu service, in my tent, at ten A. M. So, setting aside the medicine chests, tables, etc., and throwing out the sides of the tent, to make it as large as possible, we all met, and I preached from Gal. v. 13, and conducted a regular Sabbath service in Telugu, probably the first ever held in the Kadiri Taluk.

Bazaar day is on Sunday here, so, at two P. M., we went down to the market tope, and preached to large crowds, under the shade of the trees; and, at five P. M., I rode out between two and three miles, to the camp of the senior officer, where all the Europeans had assembled, and gave them an English service. I was very tired when the day's work was over.

To-day, as I expected, larger numbers of patients have come in. I began as soon as I returned from preaching this morning, and resting a couple of hours at noon, finished at five P. M., having treated 106 patients. They are beginning to come in now from the outlying villages, ten or thirteen miles off. I expect a busy day tomorrow.

Tannakal, Friday evening. I found that there was both mission and medical business, which called for my presence in Madanapalle on Wednesday. Under ordinary circumstances, I should have left Kadiri on Monday night or Tuesday morning, and made two journeys of the distance, fifty-one miles, but so many were applying for treatment in Kadiri, that I could not find it in my heart to run off on Tuesday morning. So, borrowing a couple of ponies, and sending my own, and one of them on in advance, I waited until I had treated 123 patients, and then started, and made one pull of the journey to

Madanapalle, reaching there horseback about midnight. I was pretty well shaken with the long ride, one of the ponies I had borrowed being a hard rider, and the roads very rough. Being in Madanapalle on Wednesday, gave me the opportunity to deliver the Wednesday evening Biblical lecture to educated Hindus, in the "Free Reading Room." When I am near enough, I often ride in for that, as I always have a good audience of attentive listeners. Finishing up my work in Madanapalle, I came back here, thirty-six miles, yesterday, my tents having, in the meantime, been moved from Kadiri, to this place.

The first group of sick that appeared this morning, before sunrise, was from ten miles beyond Kadiri. By the time they had heard of my being in Kadiri, and come there, I had left, so they followed me on here, fifteen miles, and another company came in from Kadiri at noon. I have had some very interesting audiences to preach to to-day, and have enjoyed my work.

Saturday. I went out preaching this morning, and was back at my medical work by 7:30 A. M., and worked on, stopping an hour for breakfast, until the market had begun, (this being market day,) when I went out, with my native helpers, and preached to different groups until four P. M. Had a discussion with some Brahmans, who wanted to prove to the people that their way was the best, after all, lest they should be left without followers and without support. After the bazaar was over, I came back and treated a few more patients at my tent.

Sunday. Blessed day of rest, but it has proved to me a blessed day of work, instead of rest, work for the Master, who hesitated not to heal on the Sabbath day. I have had to-day 110 patients from some twenty different villages, some of them fifteen and twenty miles off, villages among the hills to the west, that we could never hope to visit, and where, perhaps, the message of salvation would never have been heard by the present generation, if it had not been for some of them finding their way here for medical treatment. We have not gone to the villages preaching to-day, but have confined ourselves to preaching to the successive groups of patients, and many have taken back with them Scripture portions and tracts, that may guide them to the port of peace.

Chikatimanupalle, Christmas evening. This has proved one of the hardest day's work I have had. Off among the hills, nine miles northeast of Tannakal, is the little market town of Kokanti. To-day was the market day, so I sent off two of the native helpers, at daylight, to that place, with a supply of tracts and books, promising to follow them myself, in time for the bazaar. My tent was to be moved on to this place, seven miles, to-day. This is also nine miles from Kokanti, it being at the apex of a triangle, with a base of seven miles on the main road, and my tent was to be moved along this base, while I went on to the market at Kokanti.

I had told the people, at Tannakal, that I would treat all who came, up till nine o'clock. Knowing I was going to leave, patients poured in early, so that, at sunrise, when I began to work, there was already quite a crowd, and although, after I had preached, I went on examining and prescribing for patients, as fast as possible, having two assistants to dispense the medicine, the people came faster than I could attend to them, and, at eight o'clock, there was a crowd of 200 around my tent. I stopped and preached again, and then resumed my work. They were evidently afraid that I would leave before I had treated all, and so pressed upon one another, each trying to get in first, that I had to put up stakes in front, with but one entrance, and place a guard to let in but one at a time. By 11:45, however, I had got through with them all, 124 patients, the rest being friends accompanying them.

I then had breakfast, and at 12:15 mounted my pony, and rode off, nine miles over the hills, to Kokanti, reaching that place at two o'clock. I found the catechists already at work in the market, and, joining them, I, myself, preached to seven different audiences, aiding in selling books between the addresses. I continued working thus, in the bazaar, till 4:20, when I mounted my pony, and started for this place, Chikatimanupalle, nine miles. The sun was very hot, and the wind was so high that I could not hold an umbrella, and, as the sun shone on my back, I felt as though it were blistered. By the time I had gone a little way, what with my 124 patients, and preaching in the morning, my ride to Kokanti in the sun, and seven addresses to open-air audiences in the bazaar, I felt pretty well done up, so much so, that, before I had gone many miles, I got off my pony, and lay down by the roadside to rest, before I could summon up resolution to proceed. However, I got here about dark, and found my dinner waiting for me, my carts having come up some two hours before. After dinner, and a good cup of tea, I felt refreshed, and so ends my Christmas day. Christmas holidays surely! But how could one better keep the day, or better please Him whose birth is to-day celebrated, than by making His name and birth and saving power known to hundreds of those, who had never before even heard of Him? O may He give me grace and strength, to enable me to make the most of this glorious opportunity of making His salvation known. Combining the medical with Evangelistic work on tours, makes hard work for the missionary, but it pays.

Kandukur, Wednesday. I came on here yesterday. This is a large market town, and is noted as being the worst fever region in all the district. The drinking water is very bad, and almost every other man you meet, has either fever, or its result "ague cake," or enlarged spleen. The fevers here are mostly of the quartan type, coming on every fourth day. There are many here who have had it for more than twelve months with the omission of scarcely a single turn. It is a very persistent form of fever, and prevails all over the region in which I have been touring, but this is its headquarters. I have had hundreds of cases of it to treat at my dispensary at Madanapalle, and I have found, that almost the only way to conquer it, is to give hypodermic injections of quinine. This method of administration has been pronounced by many to be unsafe, unscientific, and barbarous, but I am able to point to nearly 1,000 cases, treated by the hypodermic injection of quinine within the last five or six years, and my experience proves it to be safe, eminently successful, and more permanent in its results, than when the quinine is taken by the mouth. I find, moreover, that it saves fully three-fourths of the quinine, *i. e.*, it requires less than one-fourth the quantity, when injected under the skin, than when swallowed to produce a permanent cure. The natives see its good results, and have great faith in it. A group of men came to me to-day, having followed me all the way from Kadiri, to have their "arms pricked," as they call it, for quartan fever, and they reported, that not a patient whose arm I had "pricked" when there, has had any return of the fever.

I usually inject four grains, dissolved in twenty drops of distilled water, by the aid of hydrochloric acid. I have injected twenty cases to-day, and upward of 200 during the last six weeks. On another tour I injected seventy in one day. We have had, to-day, large audiences of Brahmans and merchants to preach to, and have found good sale for our books.

Tippasamudram. Plenty of work again to-day. Before leaving Kandukur at 12:30, I had treated sixty-seven patients, including one important surgical operation. Riding five miles, I came to a market tope, and spent the time till four P. M., preaching to successive audiences, and then came on here, three miles farther, reaching this place before my tent came up from Kandukur. However, it soon arrived, and I got it pitched soon after dark, and have now, 8:30 P. M., just had my dinner, and must have prayers with my native helpers, and then be off to bed. Judging from the number of men who came to me in the market to-day, asking for advice, I shall have a busy day to-morrow.

Friday. On rising this morning, before sunrise, I found a crowd of people already waiting for me. They had followed me from Kadiri, being too late for me at each of my previous encampments. Soon another company came up from Tannakal, and another from Chikatimanupalle, and still another, from a village close to Kandukur. Before I had done with these, the people of the town began to pour in, and, except while at breakfast, I have hardly had any intermission all day long. As I was closing up at night, another group of six patients came up, dusty and foot-sore, having travelled forty miles to find me, or from ten miles beyond Kadiri. Four of them were quartan fever cases.

I have been in this fever region so long now, and have had so much work to do in the sun, that I have had a chill and fever myself, almost every day of late. I have taken large doses of quinine, but without effect, and have now given myself a hypodermic injection, and hope to have no farther trouble. I have had a great many cases of blindness brought to me to-day. I restored sight to two blind people lately, by operating for cataract, and, hearing of this, there have overtaken me to-day, quite a number of cases of blindness, some of them perfectly hopeless from staphyloma, and other causes. A few, however, are cases of simple cataract, and I shall get the men to come to my hospital at Madanapalle next week for operation. I have had 108 patients to-day.

Kotta Kóta, Saturday evening. I rode on here at daylight this morning, and preached in the main street of the town on my arrival. There does not seem to be so much sickness here, as at my former camps, still, as many patients as I could well attend to, have come in during the day.

Sunday. To-day is Bazaar day here, and an incident has occurred which has interested and encouraged us. We were out as far as this a year ago, and were here on Bazaar day, and sold nearly 200 Scriptures and tracts. To-day, as Catechist Souri had just concluded preaching to his first audience, a man of high caste stepped out from the crowd and said, "Yes, this is the true religion; last year I heard these people preach here, and bought one of their 'Spiritual Teachings,' and the study of that has made me cease worshipping idols, and I now pray only to Jesus Christ; just see what a beautiful prayer there is at the end of the book," and he repeated it from memory, and explained sentence by sentence. "I now see," he said, "what a beautiful and soul-satisfying prayer that is, I shall pray it every day till I die, and I advise all of you to buy these books and judge for yourselves." The once preaching in the bazaar last year, and this one little book purchased there, were all the means of grace this man had enjoyed, but he seemed fully in earnest, travelling the heavenly road.

Monday evening, New Year's day. Home

again! I rode in this morning from our last camp, thirty-two miles off, preaching once on the way. This ends our tour of twenty-nine days. We have, while out, visited nine market towns on their Bazaar day, and preached and sold Scriptures and books to audiences assembled from hundreds of villages. We have preached in seventy-eight different villages, and have sold 1,013 Scriptures, books, and tracts.

During this tour, I have treated 713 different patients, giving each patient an average of five days' treatment. These patients came from 130 towns and villages, and to all the Word of Life was preached. The 1,013 books sold to the patients and in the weekly markets, have, at the least calculation, found their way to 100 villages; may the life-giving Spirit accompany these books, and cause, that each being read, understood and believed, may bring forth fruit unto everlasting life. I have given this chapter of experience to show how we combine medical, evangelistic and colporteur work. Such work is not in vain.

X

HINDUISM AS IT IS

MODERN Hinduism, the Hinduism held and practiced by the people of India for the last 2,000 years, and held by them still, is not at all the religion of the Védas. That was essentially a pure monotheism.

The Védas, dating back from near the time of Moses, before all Noachian tradition had vanished from among men, contain in the main true ideas of God and man and sin and sacrifice. They teach of one Supreme Being, the creator, preserver and governor of all; that He is pure and holy; that man is in a state of sin, not at peace with holy God; that sinful man can have no union with sinless God until and unless sin is in some way expiated. But they fail to show how this expiation is to be accomplished, and leave the devotee groping in uncertainty and dread.

The Aryans brought these monotheistic Védas with them when they migrated into North India. But there soon arose another series of religious books, the Upanishads, commentaries on the

Védas, rituals, all those books known to the Hindus as "The Shástras." These are theoretically held to be of only secondary authority to the Védas; but, in reality, it is they, with the still later books, "The Puránas," that teach the religion, and control the lives of the Hindus of the present age.

With them first came in the idea of the Hindu Triad, and the host of minor gods; of Nirvána, or final absorption; of caste distinctions and caste observance. Modern polytheism and idolatry; pilgrimages to holy places; desert wanderings and asceticism; physical tortures; infant marriages; virgin widowhood; suttee, or the burning of a widow on the funeral pyre of her departed lord, all crept in under the shadow of these Shástras and Puránas.

Hinduism, since before the time of Christ, holds to The *Trimúrti*, that is, the Hindu Triad, Brahma, Vishnu, and Siva. Brahma being the Creator, Vishnu the preserver, and Siva the destroyer. Brahma, their books tell us, committed incest; was guilty of such lustful conduct that he was cursed to the effect that no temple should ever be built in his honour, and no knee should ever bow to him in worship, and to this day, although India is filled with Hindu temples, there is nowhere one erected to Brahma, and he has no worshippers.

The Hindus are nearly equally divided between the worshippers of Vishnu, or Vaishnavites and the worshippers of Siva, or Saivites. One party, with the trident on their foreheads, painted in two nearly perpendicular lines of white, converging toward the bridge of the nose, with a perpendicular line of red between them, range themselves under Vishnu as the Supreme God. The others, with three horizontal lines of sandalwood ashes smeared on their foreheads, worship Siva as the Supreme. There is a cordial animosity between these two sects, breaking out often into abuse and quarrels, and even sometimes riots.

The wife of Vishnu is Lakshmi, the goddess of beauty and fortune, and their son is Káma, the India Cupid, the God of love. The monkey is sacred to Vishnu. His temples swarm with them, and they are cared for, and bountifully fed, as the descendants and present representatives of Hanumán, the Monkey-God who assisted Ráma, one of Vishnu's incarnations, in recovering his captured wife, Síti, from Rávana, giant king of Ceylon, who had stolen her. All these are devoutly worshipped by the Vaishnavites, or followers of Vishnu.

The wife of Siva is Párvati, and their two sons are Vighnéswara or Ganésa, the remover of obstacles, or the God of all new undertakings, and Subhramania, the God of war.

The son Ganésa, is practically, far more worshipped than the father and mother. He is represented with the head and trunk of an elephant, and pot-bellied. He must be worshipped on the beginning of any and every new undertaking, and for the removal of all obstacles. His hideous image, chiseled in stone, carved in wood and in ivory, cast in copper, or brass, is found everywhere; granite ones by the roadside for convenience, and in temples; wood and metal ones in every Saivite's house.

Inferior to these are multitudes of deities who are supposed to attend to specific affairs of family life and business undertakings of every kind, as birth, betrothal, marriage, sickness, death, and hosts more of still inferior gods and goddesses, which must be worshipped and propitiated if the worshipper is to have a quiet and happy life. Indeed their books teach that there are 330,000,000 of gods, male and female, named and unnamed. Of these the Hindus stand in continual fear, and they must be continually propitiated, by libations, offerings, and sacrifices.

The temples, the roadside shrines, the groves, the highways and byways, the market-places and bazaars, and the houses, family rooms, bedrooms and kitchens, swarm with idols representing these gods, great and small, reminding them of the acts of worship they must perform.

The character of these multitudinous gods of the Hindus, from Brahma down, will not bear inspection. The morals of a people are never higher than those of the gods they worship. This accounts for the lax morality so sadly in evidence among the people of India.

Polygamy is recognized in their system, and practiced among the Telugus as among others of the Hindus. There are no "old bachelors" among them. They believe that their after condition depends in a degree on their having male offspring to perform their funeral obsequies and subsequent ceremonies. They have a proverb which says, "Get a good wife if you can; if not, get a bad one; marry you must."

If after marriage they have no children, or if they have only girls, it is, according to their teachings, incumbent on them to marry another wife. I have known a Hindu who, with four wives, had only daughters. He married a fifth in hope of having sons.

Hindus often look upon plurality of wives, however, in a somewhat different light. A Hindu gentleman of high position, who had been a patient of mine, came in from his distant home to express his thanks to me for his restored health, and to make me a friendly visit. After talking on various matters of interest he asked how many wives I had. "Only one, most assuredly," was my reply.

"What, sir," said he, "can a benevolent gentleman like yourself, so continually doing good to all around you, rest satisfied with throwing your protecting mantle over only one poor unprotected female? How can you regard that as doing your full duty toward the weaker sex?"

Boys are regarded by them as a blessing, and girls as a curse. If a boy is born they think the deity is pleased and confers a favour; if a girl, it is a sign of the divine displeasure. If a birth is announced in a friend's house, ere they send any messages they must ascertain whether it is a case calling for congratulations, a boy, or condolence, a girl. When our sixth son was born, and we had no daughter, a Hindu Rajah, whose dominions lay not far from my station, an old patient of mine, came in to congratulate me over the birth of "six sons, without a daughter to spoil it all."

I told him that both his mother and myself were much disappointed that it was not a daughter. He looked and spoke as though he considered me daft for having such a wish.

"But, your highness," said I, "where would you and I be were it not for our mothers?"

"Ah, sir," said he, "there are sinners enough in the world so that there will be no lack of women. There is no necessity for the righteous to have daughters."

The Hindu caste system is nowhere indicated in the Védas. It arose after the migration of the Aryans into India. Yet there is not a part of their religion which, for these past twenty centuries, has held such an iron grip upon the people. For it is a religious, not a social, distinction. The progenitors of each caste they hold to have been a separate creation on the part of Brahma; the Brahmans being created from his head; the Kshatryas, warriors, from his shoulders; the Vaishyas, merchants and artisans, from his loins; the Sudras, farmers, from his thighs, and labourers from his feet. There are subdivisions of these castes covering every trade and profession.

A man is born into a caste; he never can ascend. A merchant's son must be a merchant. The son of one of the blacksmith caste, a blacksmith. It stunts progress. It prevents true brotherly feeling. Under it a Brahman may rightly say, "stand by thyself, I am holier than thou." Its provisions are cast-iron, and on observing them one's future depends. I have known of a Brahman who died in sight of food placed there for his sustenance, because, forsooth, that food had been cooked by one of lower caste. "Better die," said he, "and gain heaven, than eat that food and live, and lose caste, and lose heaven."

It is one of our greatest obstacles in missionary work. The Brahmans would rather see a son die than become a Christian and disgrace their caste.

Transmigration of souls is also a doctrine of modern Hinduism nowhere indicated in the Védas. It teaches that when one dies, his soul will simply enter another body, superior or inferior to his former condition according as to whether merit or demerit has preponderated in this life. Each one hopes that his soul may, in the next birth, be born a Brahman. Each one fears that it may be born in one of lower caste, or as an animal or reptile. They hold that this transmigration will go on until finally they shall, in some way, have acquired so much merit that the soul may be absorbed into that of the Deity, and their individual existence cease. This is the *Nirvána*, or final absorption, which is the highest state of future bliss to which Hinduism points its most zealous devotees.

The stolid indifference with which most Hindus meet death, is explained by this belief, that at death they are simply passing one milestone in their almost endless series of existences, and that there is as good a chance in the next birth as in that which they are leaving.

Those who posed as representatives of Hinduism at the "Parliament of Religions," portrayed a kind of ancient Védic Hinduism, revised to suit their own ideas, and make it palatable to persons of Western culture. Culling its choicest, and giving a Christian colouring to many of its conceptions, they evolved and held up to the admiration of their credulous auditors *as Hinduism* a system as different, nay far more different from the real Hinduism of India's people since the days of Malachi than Christianity is from Mormonism.

The native newspapers of India sneer at the utterances of the Chicago representatives of Hinduism, as utterly untrue pictures of Hinduism as it exists. Indeed "*The Hindu Nation*," an orthodox leading Hindu newspaper, says:

"The pure and undefiled Hinduism which Swâmi Vivékánanda preached has no existence to-day; has had no existence for centuries." And "*The Reis and Rayyet*," another representative Hindu paper, adds, "In fact abomination worship is the main ingredient of modern Hinduism."

And yet the mass of the Hindus suppose that the Hinduism of to-day has come down to them from the Védas, for not one man in ten thousand in India really knows what the Védas teach, but are simply satisfied to take their religion as it comes to them from their immediate fathers.

In spite, however, of the trammels of their superstition and the blind teachings of their Shástras, many Hindus do have a sense of the burden of sin, and a desire for its expiation, and a longing for conformity to, and communion with a personal God and father, and do have an undefined hope of a future world of bliss.

This we see indicated in the writings of their sages and poets of all the ages. This we find now and then in the thoughtful Hindus of the present day. This gives us an invaluable leverage in gaining access to their hearts and presenting Jesus Christ as the all-sufficient Saviour from sin, its pollution, its penalty; as the one who can lift us up to become sons of God.

XI

"LORD GANÊSA" AND LITTLE RÁMASWÁMI

I SAW a sight one day that made my heart ache, ache for the boys and girls of India, and which I desire to picture to the boys and girls of the dear home lands, to see if they will not lend a vigorous hand in soon making such things impossible in all of idol-ridden India.

I was walking down the main street of the great heathen city of Madras toward the temple of the god Ganésa. It stood right on the street, and was not larger inside than a hall bedroom, for the Hindus do not assemble in these wayside temples for worship, but go in, one or two at a time, to present their offerings to the god of the temple.

At the farther end of the temple, on a stone platform as high as a table, and facing the wide-open front doors, was the god Ganésa. He has an elephant's head and trunk, and a huge belly, and was chiselled out of stone, sitting on a large stone rat, and as tall as a man. He was very black and shiny from the ghee, or melted butter, poured over his head by the worshippers, to make him feel good-natured and so grant their requests, and had garlands of white flowers around his neck, placed there by some worshipper.

As I neared the temple I came upon a Hindu mother taking her little son Râmaswâmi, to make his first offering to the god Ganésa in that temple. On his arms were hanging garlands of flowers and in his hands was incense to offer. He was chatting merrily, in Tamil, with his mother, who had hold of his hand and was telling him how he must go into the temple, making his salaams and showing his offerings, and then place them in the god's lap with his own hands, so that the god would always be his friend and not harm him.

As they came in front of the wide-open door, little Râmaswâmi saw the huge black idol, with his eyes painted to look fierce, his tusks white and sticking out toward him, his tongue fiery red, and his black trunk raised up to one side as if to strike. With a scream he pulled his hand away from his mother's and sprang to one side, out of sight of the monster, and stood trembling with fright. His mother, laughing at his terror, reassured him, saying, "The god won't strike you; he is a good god and likes to have little boys worship him. Come and lay your offerings in his

A HINDU FUNERAL SCENE

A TEMPLE ELEPHANT

lap, Rámaswámi, don't be afraid;" and led him again up to the side of the door.

As soon as he came in front of the horrid idol he screamed again, and tearing away from his mother, ran down the street toward his home. The mother, with a hard laugh, overtook him half a block away, seized him and half dragged him back to the temple, and said,

"You little fool! Is your father's son going to be a coward? The god won't strike you. He won't harm you. Don't you see, he is made of stone and can't move; he can't hurt you. Come along, you little imp, and lay your flowers and incense in his lap;" and pushing the screaming child before her, with one hand firmly grasping each shoulder, she forced him, in terror as he was, up onto the steps before the idol and made him lay the offerings in the lap of the god.

Immediately he had done this, he twisted himself from her grasp, and, without making any salaams to the god, dashed past me down the street for his home, still screaming with fright, while his mother, laughing, slowly followed him.

I lingered after they had gone, thinking of the mothers and the children in my native land, and I said, "O, if all the mothers of Christendom would be as zealous in bringing their children to the blessed Jesus as are these heathen mothers in making their children worship their repellant idols, how many more strong, living Christian characters there would be, and what an added force would they constitute in bringing on speedily that day when 'the idols shall be utterly abolished,' and when 'Jesus shall reign from sea to sea.'"

XII

A BRAHMAN'S TESTIMONY

"HE was a Christian, sir, and I believe he spoke the truth," said the Brahman magistrate.

It was in 1869. I had been away from my station for some weeks, sowing seed in the outlying regions. Shortly after my return the superior magistrate of the district, a cultured English gentleman, came to call upon me one day and in the course of the conversation, he said, "I have something to tell you, which I think will please you." "Have you," said I, "then please tell it."

He told me of a case that had been before the court of the Brahman magistrate of the town during my absence which was this:

A poor man of good caste had borrowed money of the *soucars*, or rich, high caste money-lenders, in the chief Bazaar street of the town. The money was due, and the poor man came to tell them he had failed to raise the money and asked for an extension. They refused to give it, taunted him with his poverty and said he made no effort to raise the money to pay them, and that he must in some way, raise the money and pay them immediately. He in turn complained of them as oppressors.

They flew into a rage, pounced upon him, gave him a beating, and knocked him over on a heap of granite, inflicting a number of wounds and injuries. They were somewhat startled to see the wounds as evidence of their assault, and withdrew to their banking bazaar, to consult what to do. The wounded man, saying that he would complain against them for assault, went to the house of a *Vakil*, or native lawyer, to get him to formulate the complaint in the magistrate's court. The assailants rushed directly to the magistrate, and clamorously laid charges against the injured man, that he had made an attack upon them, and that simply in defending themselves they had chanced to inflict wounds upon him, and demanded the arrest of the injured man.

As in Solomon's time, "on the side of the oppressors there was power," the injured man was arrested and charged with assault upon the *soucars*. The case came before the Brahman magistrate referred to above for trial. Each party was ordered to produce its witnesses.

The prosecuting party, the *soucars*, all appeared and told the same story; they had summoned a large number of witnesses who swore that this poor man had violently assaulted them, and that they had simply acted in self-defence, and wounded him.

No one dared to appear in behalf of the poor wounded man; one or two were summoned, who had been within sight and hearing when the assault occurred, but fearing the vengeance of the powerful clique on the other side, refused to testify, declaring they knew nothing of the case.

The simple story of the injured man, that he had himself been violently attacked, beaten and wounded by these men, and that they simply to shield themselves had brought this charge against him was unsupported by any testimony.

Here in India a powerful party can hire any number of Hindu witnesses for a quarter of a dollar each, to swear to anything they wish to have proven, but there is no sense of justice which compels a man to testify for an innocent or injured party, when he thinks he will, either socially or otherwise, be the loser thereby.

The Brahman magistrate knew not what to think; he strongly suspected that the charge made by the *soucars* was a false one, but the sworn testimony in their behalf was very strong; he knew not quite what course to take. On a little reflection he turned to a police constable who appeared on the scene just at the conclusion of the assault, asking if he knew of any one else who had seen the assault and could testify to what had really occurred.

"Yes, sir," said he, "the catechist of the American mission was standing in the main street, at the head of this Bazaar street, and appeared to have seen all that went on." His house was near at hand; the magistrate summoned him, and told him he wished his testimony as to what had really occurred.

He was put under oath, upon the Bible, and said that as he was passing by in the main street on his way to the hospital that morning, to obtain medicine for his sick wife, he had heard an altercation and stopping to see what it meant, he had seen these three *soucars* spring from their seat in the veranda of their bazaar, upon this man, who now stood as defendant, and give him a beating and knock him violently on to an adjacent heap of stones, and told in detail all that had passed. He was cross-questioned, but his simple statement remained unbroken. The magistrate sent to the hospital and found that at the hour named the catechist had appeared at the hospital to obtain medicine as he had stated.

The case against the poor man was dismissed. The prosecutors were charged with assault upon the poor man, convicted and sentenced to punishment.

"The records of the case in full," said the English magistrate, "came before me for perusal and for revision, if I saw cause. I read the case with all the testimony very carefully. The next day the Brahman magistrate called and I said to him, 'How is it that with so many witnesses testifying so strongly in favour of the prosecution, and very little more than this one witness for the defence, you dismiss their case, and proceed against the accusers?' The native magistrate replied, 'These men seemed to me to be bearing false witness. Their testimony looked as though they had all been instructed just what to say. I believed they were hired to swear to what they did. But, this man was a Christian, and I believe he spoke the truth.' And in looking over the case," said the English magistrate, "I think that the native magistrate was right, and the conviction of the accusers stands."

"I told you this," said the superior magistrate, "for I think it will encourage you in your work, to know that even non-Christian officials regard the Christians as worthy of belief because they are Christians."

It did encourage me, and it encourages me more as I look over the country and see the growing feeling among all classes, that the religion of Jesus does elevate those who truly embrace it, to a higher level of morality, and a nobler stand in all that is good.

There are many now everywhere who are ready to reiterate the Brahman's declaration, "He was a Christian and I believe he spoke the truth."

XIII

A DAYBREAK AUDIENCE AND A CHASE FOR A TIGER

It was three weeks after the angry mob had heard and melted at the Story of The Cross. We, myself and four native assistants, had come on more than a hundred miles farther north in the kingdom of Hyderabad. Yesterday had occurred the incidents given in "The Man with the Wonderful Books" as recounted in the preceding volume. We had, on that afternoon preached for eight hours, from two to ten P. M., to an ever-growing audience of people hastily gathered from many villages. One of us at a time had gone away to rest, and eat, while the others were setting forth anew, and with more and more incidents, the life and work and power and mercy of "the God Man" who had appeared on earth for man's salvation, and supplying them with "The History of the Divine Guru"—the gospels—and with booklets explaining them, which they had eagerly purchased for one *dub* each. At ten o'clock we had told them that we must lie down and rest now as we were very weary with our long journey of the morning, and with our continued preaching of the afternoon and evening, and must now get some sleep, for we must be again on our way at daylight, and they reluctantly withdrew.

On our arrival at near noon, they had taken us to a small, granite built Hindu temple in a tope, or grove, fronting their village, and bidden us put up in that, for if those wonderful books they had before obtained and read were true, they did not want this temple and these gods any more. They had themselves assisted in taking our things into the temple, placing my folding traveller's cot where, as I lay resting while my breakfast was preparing, I could reach out my hand and lay it on the chief idol and say, Yes, this is one of those of which it is said, in my Book of Instructions, "The idols He shall utterly abolish." We had not therefore pitched our tents nor unloaded them from the carts.

At eleven o'clock, when the last of the people had gone, and we had had our evening prayers, we lay down to sleep in the portico of the temple, for it was too hot and close to sleep inside. Too much interested in and excited by the events of the preceding day, I slept but little. As my eyes opened, along through the night watches, toward the streets of the village, I could see unusual lights burning, way on until dawn. At the first break of day we arose and put our beds, luggage and boxes of books upon our carts, to start upon another day's march and another day's preaching. Until a fortnight before we had been wont to start considerably earlier, but since we entered this jungly, sparsely populated region, so infested with ravenous beasts, prudence had required that we wait until the daylight had driven them back to their lairs.

Just as we were starting, a group of people from the village came up, saying, "Sirs, this is such strange news, and so good if true, that we have been reading these books all night to see if there were anything in them which we did not understand, so that we could ask your explanation before you went on, for we may never see a missionary again." And one of them opened a gospel, with leaves turned down here and there, and began asking questions, while all listened eagerly for the reply. Seeing that it would take some time to answer all their questions, and thinking that as the sun was now soon to rise, all danger from ravenous beasts was past, I proposed to my native associates to go on with the equipment, as we wished to reach the next village, some five miles ahead, before the people had gone out to the fields to work, and saying that I would answer these questions and then canter on rapidly and overtake them. They went on. I turned to answer the questions, but so many leaves were turned down, and so earnestly did they ask question after question, that it was fully three-quarters of an hour before I could get away.

The last question they asked was one I could not answer. They had, after many questions about incidents in the gospels, and about the character and the claims of the God Man, asked as to where it was that He became man, and was born a babe, and whether He were a white man, or like them. I had told them that in a land midway between their country and the land of the white Christians, and among Asiatic people, much like themselves, with a similar dress and customs and of a complexion between theirs and mine, among a people especially prepared of the great God for His advent, this Son of God had taken on human form for our redemption. They seemed pleased that He was more like them than we foreigners, and asked,

"How long ago did this happen?" I told them the number of centuries, and how He had commanded His disciples to go into all the world and preach this gospel to every creature and how, in process of time, the good news had reached the western lands, and they all had become Christians, and how now, because His love burned in their hearts, they had sent me and many others to come to their land and learn their language and give them the glad news.

"Sir, did you say that this Yésu Krístu (Jesus Christ) came into the world and did all this more than 1,800 years ago?"

"Yes," said I.

"Sir, if this be true why have you Christians not told us of it before?" I could not answer that question. I wonder if any one who reads this can answer it.

At last bidding them a loving farewell and commending them to Him of whom so late they had heard, I mounted my horse and hastened to follow my people.

There were no roads in that region. We had guides to show us the most feasible path from village to village. For parts of our journey we had low narrow carts with wheels of solid wood cut from the trunk of a large tree, and with buffaloes to draw them. In other places everything had to be carried on the heads of coolies. Here we had carts. The guides were conducting the party along the sandy, dry bed of a crooked little stream on the upper banks of which the next village was built. I struck the stream and cantered up it to overtake our party. As usual I kept a sharp watch of the path and of the bushes at the sides.

I had not gone a quarter of a mile before I caught sight of the tracks of a very large tiger, the largest tiger tracks I had ever seen. We had been in the tiger jungle now for two weeks. On the path over which we had passed the preceding day seven people had recently been killed and eaten by these "Man Eaters" as tigers that have tasted human blood are called. We had kept blazing camp-fires around our tent by night for ten days. But on a bright day, especially a bright morning, the tigers usually keep in the jungle, coming out by day when it is cloudy or toward nightfall. The sun was now up and shining brilliantly. What could this mean? I sprang from my horse and kneeled down to examine the tracks and see whether they had been made before or after our party had passed. There they were, planted squarely over the track of the last cart, and evidently following it.

The mystery was explained, for, along by the side of the big tracks, I now found the small tracks of a tiger cub. It was an old mother tiger, who, hampered with the care of her cub, had not been able to get her prey during the night and who, in spite of the sun, was now out searching for breakfast for herself and child. She was following the carts, waiting for a chance to spring. The tigers of these jungles never spring into a crowd of people. They lurk and wait until one falls in the rear or goes to one side and then spring upon him. I saw at once the danger in which my native assistants walking with the carts were placed. So long as they kept together and close by the carts they were pretty safe. Should one of them stop to quench his thirst at a little rocky pool in the side of the river, or for any other purpose, Mistress Tiger would be upon him, and the little one would have its first quäff of Christian preacher's blood.

Springing onto my pony I struck the spurs into his side and dashed forward furiously. I always carried with me, in the jungle, a fourteen inch navy revolver loaded with rifle balls. I had practiced until I could bring down a squirrel or a crow with it. I knew I might not kill a tiger, but with accurate shooting I might blind or disable it, if no more, and at all events I must share the danger whatever it be, with my native associates. Could I reach them before the spring were made I might avert the danger. On I dashed for one mile. The tracks were still there. From my unusual use of the spurs my faithful horse saw there was something wrong and became excited. The second mile was covered with leaps and bounds with the pistol ready cocked in my right hand and my eye watching every bush and every rod of the river, we went flying over the third mile. In my anxiety to reach my men in time to warn and save them I could scarcely breathe. I knew I must be nearing them. The tracks big and little were still there.

Suddenly a sharp turn in the river brought the carts into sight moving along peacefully, and I could see the four native preachers, and the cook and the tent lascar walking along together, close by the carts. I knew they were safe. I had reined up my horse so they should not see me. I looked and the tracks had disappeared. Just before the bend I had seen them. The tiger had doubtless been lurking there. As it had heard the furious clatter of my horse's shoes on the gravel, as I turned the preceding bend only a few rods back, it had doubtless sprang with its cub, behind the bush on the jutting corner, which was so near as to brush my stirrup as I passed. And very likely its breath had fallen on me as I flew by at too rapid a gait for it to spring on me.

Keeping just far enough back not to attract the attention of the party in front and watching the jungle intently on both sides of the stream to see if the tiger should again appear, I lingered in the rear for some twenty minutes for my horse to cool down, for though a bay horse he was white with foam when I passed the tiger bend, and I knew that, if I joined the party in that condition, apprehension would be excited, and questions asked which it would be difficult for me to parry, for I did not want them then to know what a narrow escape they had had, as we still had 100 miles of this tiger jungle before us. Presently joining them I began at once to tell them what an interesting time I had had with the people of the last village, after they left, and what earnest questions they asked and so kept on talking until we reached the next village and were absorbed again in the work of the Master.

They never knew, until we had reached home nearly four months later, of their danger and deliverance that morning, nor of several other dangers known only to myself, through which they passed unharmed. How appropriate sounded the ninety-first psalm that night at our evening prayers in our tent, for once again we had felt the presence of the "Lo, I am with you."

XIV

THE SPOTTED TIGER FOILED

My camp was pitched in a valley between mountains towering up 4,000 feet above the sea, and 1,700 feet above my tent. I had been visiting, instructing, and encouraging the little Christian congregation there, and preaching in all the surrounding towns and villages for several days. It was necessary to move camp that day to another cluster of Christian villages on the other side of the mountain, many miles around by a tortuous route through the valleys. I had much writing to do, and did not wish to spend the time for a circuitous journey, so despatched my tent and camp equipage in the early morning, to be pitched in the new place, and sent word to the people of that cluster of villages that I would hold a meeting in the central village that evening at dusk. My pony was to meet me at the east foot of the mountain to take me three miles to my new camp.

Spending a good part of the day in the little village schoolhouse, quietly writing letters, I walked up the mountain-side in the afternoon by a footpath that I knew. Halfway up I stopped to rest under a banyan-tree, or jungle fig-tree, where, a year before, a native farmer, running down the path, had come upon an old she-bear and her cub, under this tree, eating the wild figs. The old bear, thinking he was rushing for her cub, sprang upon him, hugged him, and badly mangled his right arm until her cub had vanished in the bushes, when she left him and followed her cub. The man was brought into my hospital, and for many weeks it was a question whether he would ever regain the use of his right arm. He finally did, however, and when the English judge of the district organisêd a hunt for that bear, in which I joined, he was there to show us where the tussle had taken place, and help us find his old enemy.

There are many wild beasts inhabiting these mountain jungles: wild boar, deer, Indian elk, hyenas, jackals, wolves, an occasional striped tiger, and more spotted tigers.

The spotted tigers have spots like a leopard, but are not leopards, for they have claws like a tiger and cannot climb trees as a leopard can. In size they are between the royal tiger and the leopard. In disposition and habits they are tigers and they have a tiger's strength. A friend of mine, from an opposite hill, saw one of them spring upon a small horse, kill it, suck its blood, and then drag it to its lair in the mountain recess. The spotted tigers do far more damage in our region than the striped, as they are much more numerous. If one gets a taste of human flesh nothing else will satisfy it; but such diet soon makes it mangy, and shortens its life.

The government pays a reward for the killing of all ravenous beasts, and especially for those that are known to have killed human beings. The skins are delivered to the government official who pays the reward, and were at that time periodically sold at auction. At such a sale, which I attended and made some purchases, the skin of one spotted tiger was sold, which was certified to have killed and eaten nine men, women and children. Another had killed seven; another five; another four, and another two.

We usually carry arms through these mountain jungles, but that day I had none. I had made the ascent of 1,700 feet and, walking along the west slope of the summit for a quarter of a mile, I had crossed over to the east side of the rocky crest.

It was now one hour before sundown, of a

cloudy, drizzly afternoon. I had my double umbrella, black inside and white outside, for fending off both sun and rain, but had closed it over my hand, without clasping it, to go through a narrow opening in the bushes. I had crossed a little open grass-plot of a few rods, and was just entering a narrow footpath through the mountain jungle, that would take me down to the east foot of the mountain, where I was to meet my pony.

Suddenly a spotted tiger sprang into the path, between the bushes, and disputed passage. I saw at once what he wanted; only great hunger impels these tigers to come out during the day; he had had no breakfast, and wanted missionary meat for supper. I did not wish him to have it: I had an appointment for that evening with the people of three villages, and wished to keep it. He stood in the only path through that dense mountain jungle, glaring at me. I eyed him equally intently, and, gaining his eye, held it while I formed my plan.

It is always best if a scrimmage is to take place to be the attacking party. My old grandmother used to teach me that everything would come in use within seven years, if you only kept it. When I was a boy I had gone out among an Indian tribe in Michigan, and learned their war-whoop. I had kept it for thrice seven years, but it proved trebly serviceable then. When my plan of attack was formed, springing forward toward the tiger I raised this war-whoop, and at the same time suddenly opened my double umbrella.

What it was that could so suddenly change a perpendicular dark figure into a circular white object, and at the same time emit such an unearthly yell, the tiger did not know. He stood his ground, however, until I dashed forward and, suddenly shutting my umbrella, raised it to strike him over the head. It seemed instantly to occur to him that I was the more dangerous animal of the two, and that one of us had better run; as I did not, he did. Springing aside, over a bush, into the open ground, he made for the crest of the hill which I had just passed. The crest consisted of granite slabs and masses, thrown up perpendicularly by some convulsion of nature. From a crevice of these there had grown a banyan-tree whose branches spread out over their tops. Between the leaves and the rocks, in one place, I could see the sky through, in a circle as large as a bicycle wheel.

For this the tiger made. His spring was the neatest specimen of animal motion I had ever seen. His forepaws were stretched straight out and he had his nose between them. His hind feet were stretched equally straight, and between them his tail. Straight as an arrow he went through that opening. I knew that about twenty feet down on the other side he would strike on grassy ground, and that that slope led down to a little stream, which my path again crossed less than a quarter of a mile below. Wishing to make the subjugation complete, I scrambled up to this open place and, looking through the leaves at the side of the opening, I saw the tiger trotting down the slope, but looking around every now and then, evidently wondering whether he had done a wise thing in running away.

Putting my head with its big, white, sun hat into the opening I once more raised the war-whoop. Down he dashed again with impetuosity. Withdrawing my head until he slackened his pace, I repeated the operation, and on he dashed, and so continued, until I had seen him cross the stream, and go up into the woods on the opposite side of the valley. Then, feeling sure that I would see no more of him that day, I turned and wended my way down three miles to the foot of the hill, mounted my pony and kept my appointment.

I am thankful to say that such incidents are not common in our preaching tours. I have never known of a missionary being seriously injured by ravenous beasts or venomous reptiles. But such an incident forcibly reminds us of the protection promised in the last few verses of the gospels of Matthew and Mark, in connection with the giving of the Great Commission, and that promise is wonderfully fulfilled.

XV

THE HEAT IN INDIA: HOW I KEEP MY STUDY COOL

"THE thermometer is 102° with us. How is it with you?" says a letter lying before me. Another says: "Thermometer 107° in my office all day, and 97° in my house all night. How are you standing it?" And the paper to-day says: "Thermometer in the shade *averaged* 101½°, during the heat of the day, all last week in Madras, going as high as 108° one day."

Now, what am I to do? It is only the 28th of April, and I have my heaviest literary work, in the translating of the Bible, to do between now and July. Above 95° the brain refuses to work vigorously, and, more than that, my old friend, the jungle fever, seizes those times for his visits. If I can manage to pull the thermometer down ten degrees, I can keep the fever off, and keep my brain in a working condition. I have had to make a diligent study of this problem, and have met with some success. It may be interesting to others to know what means I take.

We are in latitude 13° north, or 800 miles

further south than the southern end of Florida. Our "hot season" begins in March, and ends in October, though we have some relief during July and August, when the sun is north of us. March is hot, April is hotter, and May is scorching. September, and part of October, too, are blistering. I have seen the thermometer at 103° on the 15th of October. It pays us, therefore, to give our attention to keeping cool here, as much as it does you to keeping warm in the winter in America. And those of us who have close literary work to do must give special attention to it.

My house is, India fashion, of one-story, but is smaller and lower than Europeans' houses usually are in this country. It consists of a row of rooms twelve feet wide, stretching on one after another, and all opening on a veranda in front. My study is the south end of the house. It is twelve by ten feet. Two ends and one side are covered with books. In the middle of each end is a door. The south side has a window, and my large study-table standing against the wall. The study-table ends against one set of book shelves and has another set on it, so that I can reach 300 volumes without leaving my chair. It has slides which pull out so as almost to enclose my chair, so that I can have fifteen volumes open under my eye as I sit in my study-chair, which stands thus almost in the centre of the room and directly between the east and west doors.

Outside of the west door is a little flat-roof bathroom, with, however, a door opening outdoors from that, on the west side, so that there is a clear sweep for the wind through from east to west and from west to east. The roof, only eight feet above my head as I sit, is of tiles, resting on palmyra rafters. We have no plastered ceilings here, but, to keep the heat from striking through the tiles on our heads, we have sheeting sewed together and stretched across where a ceiling should be. This we take down and wash, from time to time, in place of white-washing.

The low, tiled roof, however, lets the heat through unmercifully. So I have put up pillars a foot high on the eaves and the ridge, and, placing bamboos on them, have made a thick thatch roof, which not only covers the tile roof but comes down, making a veranda ten feet wide all around, thus keeping the sun off the walls. There is thus a foot of air always circulating between the two roofs, and that helps a good deal to keep my study from being heated by the sun.

How I Keep My Study Cool

"How do I cool the air in the study?" That is the best of it. We take the root of the *kuskus*, an aromatic plant, whose root, when washed and prepared, looks not unlike fine oat straw, with a refreshing odour when wet, and braid this into a screen a little larger than the door before which it is to be hung. It is fastened to the door-frame at the top, and tied out two feet at the bottom so as to be slanting. If this can in any way be kept moist, the intensely dry air at this season, in passing through it, sucks up the moisture very rapidly, and the process of evaporation cools the air some ten or twelve degrees. I have one of these over my eastern door, and one over the western, so that, which ever way the wind blows from, it must pass through one of these "kuskus tatties," as we call them. To keep them wet I contrived some years ago a self-tipping trough, which is hung on a pivot at each end just above the "tatty."

The trough is a V, with one lip shorter and more perpendicular, and the other longer and running out more horizontally. Against the wall, over one end of this, is suspended a square tub, with a faucet which allows the water to trickle into the trough. The water trickling into the trough rises slowly, spreading out on the more horizontal lip of the trough until that becomes the heaviest, and over it tips, with a splash that sends the water all over the slanting tatty.

I turn the faucet to let the water run faster or slower according to the dryness of the atmosphere. Some days it must tip once a minute to keep the tatty wet. To-day, as I sit writing, it tips only once in three minutes, as the air is not so dry. It takes only twelve to fifteen gallons of water to keep one going all day, and that, in a dry day, will reduce the temperature of the room from ten to twelve degrees, and the whole thing is exceedingly inexpensive. Two dollars covers the outlay for the two doors. But wait a moment, while I take my douche, for my head is feeling oppressed; the wind has lulled, and the air is not so cool as it was half an hour ago.

There, I have had my head douche, and my brain is relieved again. It has taken me one minute, but the time is not lost. Some of these hot days I could not get on without it and do any considerable mental work. "What is this douche?" I will tell you. Hanging up over the bathtub, in my bathroom, is a porous water jar, made of clay and baked without glazing, and holding about four gallons. The water oozes through all its pores, and the evaporation from the entire external surface cools the water to some fifteen to twenty degrees below the surrounding atmosphere. I have just tried the thermometer in it. It stands at 74°, which is ten degrees cooler than the water was when drawn from the well and put in it this morning. Over the edge of this water jar—or pitcher, as it is called in the Bible—hangs a bent tube syphon. I bend my head over the tub and under the syphon, and start the water. It runs, cool and refreshing, on to the back of the head and neck, cooling the brain and shriveling up the congested blood-vessels, and giving immense relief. My hair I keep shingled to about half an inch in length, and this retains considerable moisture to evaporate in the next half hour or so and keep up the cooling process. I come back and sit down in my punka chair, and my head feels almost cold for a little time, and I begin to think of icebergs.

My punka chair is a comfort. I found that in my Bible translation work, where I have to have so many versions, ancient and Oriental, and so many dictionaries and books of reference open, that I could not get on at all with an ordinary India punka, which hangs from the ceiling, is pulled by a coolie outside, by a rope running through the wall, and stirs all the air in the room, blowing over the pages of the books, and fluttering the papers on one's table. So some years ago I devised a little punka to be attached to an ordinary cane-seat rocking-chair, so that a slight motion of the chair keeps the punka in motion directly over one's head. As I sit up straight in the chair, the punka-frill just touches my hair as it swings back and forth. It cools the head and does not disturb the books and papers, and costs nothing to work.

If the hair is kept moist, its cooling effect is marvellous, and the motion of the chair is so slight, that I write with ease, with my paper lying on the table, as I now am doing, and the punka in full swing.

With these contrivances I fight the hot weather through the season, and manage to do a fair amount of work. Without them I would be utterly prostrated with such work. It is the hottest hour of the day now, but I am holding the thermometer on my study-table below 90° and intend to continue to do so "all summer."

XVI

ODDITIES OF TRAVEL IN INDIA

"BOY, have you put my valise and bag in the coach?" "Yes, sir, done put, sir." "Are the mattresses and pillows in?" "Yes, sir." "And the luncheon box?" "Yes, sir." "And my sun umbrella, and revolver, and pith hat, and boots?" "All done put, sir."

The "boy" is a grey-haired man, but that makes no difference; for the general servant, who does the work of a butler, in India is called "boy," even though he be a Methusaleh. It is his business to see that everything is put in the coach, ready for a journey but it does not do to trust him too confidingly, or you will find, after you are well on your journey, that he has forgotten some essential thing. So you must yourself ask after each thing you wish to take.

"Have the bullocks and driver come?" "Yes, sir, done hitched to the coach." "Are you sure the order for posting bullocks was sent on all right?" "Yes, sir, I took the order to the *tahsildar* myself, and while I was there he started a *peon* on ahead with it, sir."

There are 12,000 miles of railways in India, but India is 3,000 miles long, and over 1,500 broad in places, and there is no railway station within twenty miles of one-twentieth of the population as yet. Many important towns are still fifty, or 100 miles distant from any railway.

I am just off for a journey of 400 miles, to get a little breathing spell on one of the mountain ranges in the Madras presidency, and have to travel sixty miles to the nearest railway station. For such trips we have to indent on the all-enduring *bullocks* of the country. Horses, in South India, are too expensive a luxury for long journeys. The climate is against them. Good horses have to be imported, and, like other foreigners, they easily succumb to the heat. We have to keep them for use in the towns, and about our daily work, but they are very rarely used for long journeys in the Madras presidency. Palanquins were formerly much used, but with the good military roads which the British government in India have made through the country, they have been mostly replaced by wheeled vehicles. Each European resident is expected to keep his own travelling-coach, and, whenever he wishes to take a journey, he sends word beforehand to the *tahsildar*, or county magistrate, as to the route

ASCENDING THE PULNEY MOUNTAINS

TAPPING PALMYRA TREES FOR TODDY

he wishes to go, and the time he expects to start, and orders are sent on in advance to have relays of trotting bullocks ready on the road at from six to eight miles apart, each yoke of bullocks being accompanied by its own driver, who is often the owner of the bullocks.

As often as you come to the end of a stage, you pay the driver at the rate of six or nine cents per mile, for the distance he has come, according to the official way-bill which he presents, and so you go on, by night and day, to the end of your journey. In the hot weather, however, travelling is always done in the night when practicable, to avoid the heat, and because the bullocks will travel faster by night.

The usual travelling coach, or "gharry," is a sort of two-wheeled omnibus, with a platform across the seats, and a mattress covering the whole, for night travel, and a place for luggage underneath. More recently, however, lighter four-wheeled vehicles are coming into use. The one I go in is somewhat like a "Jersey rockaway," or a green grocer's wagon, with standing cover, and oilcloth curtains which button down tight, even in front, when desired, so as to keep out all rain in the Monsoon. There are two seats, the front flap of the hind one opening up and hooking on to the front one, and its flap hooking on to the dashboard, so as to make a level surface about six feet by three inside. On this a mattress, or cushions are spread, with pillows, and two persons, if necessary, can lie, and sleep through the night, as much as the joltings and frequent changes of bullocks will allow. Under the seats is a place for luggage.

This is of a miscellaneous character, for there are no hotels on the ordinary routes of travel; only "Traveller's Bungalows," or rest-houses, unfurnished, or with simply beds, chairs, tables, and crockery. The traveller must take his lunch box, well filled, and other necessaries along with him, and usually his servant to cook rice and curry for him at the bungalows, and attend to his wants on the journey. One is never safe starting on a long journey without his sun umbrella, made of two thicknesses, white without and black within, and his pith topi or sun hat; for he may break down at midday, and have to walk miles to the nearest rest-house.

The clock strikes 9 P. M. "Boy! It is time we were off. Put in the *Kusa* (porous goglet) of cold water, and light the coach lamps, or is it bright enough moonlight to do without?" "Yes sir, done got Kusa in. White moonlight. Lamps not need. All ready, sir." "Very well. Jump on behind." And off we go.

There is a seat on behind for a servant, with a strap for him to strap himself in, lest he fall off in his sleep. The driver sits on the carriage pole, for the double purpose of putting weight on the bullocks' necks to hold down the light yoke, which is only a round pole, with ropes for bows, and also that he may be in a position to twist the bullocks' tails with his bare toes to make them quicken their gait! This he does frequently, as easier and more efficacious than whipping. The bullocks jog along at about four miles an hour. This driver has good bullocks (they are his own) and has obtained the privilege of taking me two stages, or fifteen miles, so as to earn more money. He should be at the changing place at half-past twelve.

We soon pass out from among the rice fields, which surround the town, and pass the few sugar-cane fields, and the more numerous millet fields, now all bare and parched, out into the open stony country, and on into the ten miles of open jungle we have to cross to come to the next village. Between my naps I am sure I hear the "boy" snoring on the seat behind, and think I detect, every now and then, symptoms of the driver taking short naps, when suddenly I hear a thud, and the wheels on the right side of the carriage seem to go over a big stone, or rather some large, soft obstacle. I spring up and look out under the partly rolled up curtains just in time to see the brawny driver picking himself up and shaking off the dust. The driver's seat on the pole is very small. He had got to sleep, and was nodding, and nodded so far over to the right, as he sat sideways, as to precipitate himself whack onto the ground, frightening the bullocks which jumped forward and both wheels of the light conveyance passed over his body.

He was thoroughly ashamed that he had got to sleep while on duty and tumbled off, and was afraid it would ruin his credit as a driver if it were known. I said nothing until he had limpingly caught up, and jumped on to his seat again without the bullocks having stopped, and then I said, "Well, you nodded yourself off, didn't you? I hope the wheels did not seriously hurt you." "Oh, no," said he, for he did not know that I had seen it all, "I have not been asleep. I didn't tumble off. I dropped my whip, and just jumped off and ran back to pick it up. That was all!" When, half an hour later, we came to the relay of bullocks and he was limping around unhitching his, he explained that "driving in the night sometimes gave him lumbago or rheumatism, and made him stiff and lame!" And this story he will doubtless tell his people, when he gets home, to account for his sudden lameness, so as not to be laughed at for getting to sleep and tumbling off his seat. Poor fellow; he was sufficiently punished, and I shall not tell on him. I paid him his full hire, and a present besides, to procure liniment to apply to his lumbago!

In the next nineteen miles I had three changes of bullocks and drivers. One of the other drivers tumbled off when it was not his own fault. We were passing through another somewhat open jungle. The moon was just setting, and was obscured by the clouds in the horizon, casting a faint, lurid light. The bullocks were going along quietly. The carriage made scarcely any noise to give warning of our approach. All at once a hyena, which had been crouching behind a bush, startled by our approach, darted out and across our pathway and wheeled and ran to our rear. The bullocks, terrified by the sudden apparition, dashed off. The driver lost control of them, though he had hold of the rope reins which are attached to a ring in the nose of each bullock. They sprang to the opposite side of the road from which the hyena had gone. One of the bullocks fell into a deep gutter that he was too blinded by terror to notice, and the other bullock head over heels on top of him, while the driver was pitched forward and fell partly between the prostrate oxen. No great harm was done. The ropes, which attached the yoke to the pole of the carriage, were soon repaired. The driver was unhurt, but this time it was the bullock that limped through the rest of its stage.

By six o'clock in the morning we had come thirty-four miles, and arrived at the Bungalow where I spend as much of the heat of the day as I can spare from my journey. My servant prepares a hasty "Chota hazri," or early breakfast, and I put my carriage mattress on a cot, and get some of the sleep that I did not succeed in getting during the night. With the aid of my lunch box a good dinner is made ready by two o'clock, for I must be off soon after three, to catch the train that passes the nearest railway station, twenty-six miles from here, at 10 P. M.

Whew! How hot it is, as I emerge from the shady bungalow compound out into the dusty street. It is only the middle of April, but all vegetation seems killed, except the leaves of the trees, and they look as though they were going into a decline! Fields, pastures, meadows,—not a particle of green upon one of them. Grass roots have to be dug for the horses to eat, although they live chiefly on a kind of grain called gram, a small bean. The unhappy cows and milch buffaloes wander around in the desperate attempt to find some bit of half dried up grass they can pick, and looking forward longingly for the fodder of the last crop's millet straw, which they will have as they come up to their master's house to be milked at night. The sheep are partially happy, and the multitudinous flocks of goats entirely so as they crop the leaves of the stunted bushes in the dried up jungles. The hens go panting around, with the mouth half open to breathe, vainly searching for the grasshoppers that cannot now find enough to support life, and waiting for the sundown to bring the ants out for them to prey upon. April and May are, indeed, the dreariest, deadest months of the whole year. There is the dreariness of winter, with the heat of a furnace. There is not a cloud in the brazen sky. Not a breath of air to blow away the choking dust which the bullocks kick up as they go. My black coat is fast becoming white, and the heat in the carriage seems stifling.

Over the carriage cover and sides is a covering of a double thickness of white cloth to intercept as much as possible of the sun's direct rays, but still I only exist, rather than live, until the haze of the horizon deadens the rays of the setting sun.

As darkness begins to come on I am in a mountain pass, through which a carriage road bears witness to much engineering skill. For five miles there is not the sign of a human habitation, except that near the entrance is a strongly built police station, with its armed squad of police, placed there to protect travellers from the *Dacoits,* or robber banditti, proclaimed outlaws, who, every now and then traverse this region on their marauding expeditions. The police mildly suggest to me that it would be safer if I would stop over at the police station until near morning, as native travellers usually do, but I point to my well-loaded revolver, which lies on my mattress at my side, and tell the driver to go on.

These Dacoits are unspeakably cruel in torturing their unarmed victims until they will point out their valuables secreted in their baggage, but when it comes to cold lead from a European revolver, used by a fearless foreigner, they are great cowards. It is well known that we always go armed through such places, and the knowledge of this fact mostly prevents our having to use our weapons, for it prevents our being attacked. I have taken the precaution, however, to engage in advance a *Masalji-Wallah*, or torch bearer, to run through this dark pass with his flaming torch in front of the bullocks. The Dacoits like to approach and attack in total darkness, and besides, where torches are borne in advance of a conveyance, it is probable that there are armed Europeans in the conveyance. I pass over the ground unmolested, and reach the railway station in ample time, secure a place in a sleeping compartment, and start on at a pace somewhat more rapid than that of the oxen.

It is now morning, and I am writing in the train. I have had a very funny time of it since three o'clock, but of that and of the further events of the journey I must write after I have given a description of our train and the India railway arrangements.

What a sensation this train that I am travelling on would make if seen running from New York to Philadelphia and Chicago, especially if people along the line were told that it was not an emigrant train, but the great express and mail train!

This road, "The Madras Railway," is reckoned one of the principal roads in India. It has nearly 800 miles of line, and is well built, with good stations all along the line. It is a broad guage railway, and is subsidised by the Anglo-Indian government so as to be controlled by them for military purposes. The cars are built more the shape of American freight cars, only not quite so long. They have no platforms at the ends, but are coupled together like an American freight train. Each car is divided into compartments, entered at the side of the car, and reaching across. The seats face one another, and each single compartment holds twelve persons when crowded full, one half of them riding backward.

The train is made up of three kinds of passenger carriages, besides freight and baggage cars. The first-class passenger carriages, though of the shape described above, and with doors and windows in the side only, are better built than the others, and are all arranged so as to turn into sleeping cars at night. They are cushioned with leather-covered hair cushions, but not usually with spring seats. The second-class carriages have *no* cushions, simply board seats. Shelves are made to raise up, like the shelves of a pantry, three on each side, one above another, so that six passengers can lie down comfortably, if they have brought along their own mattresses and pillows, in each compartment. If there are more than six in one compartment some must sit up. The third-class carriages are, many of them, all in one compartment, with fixed wooden benches, and with no glass windows at the sides, simply rough venetians to slide up and down; nothing to keep out dust, and no double roof. The first and second-class carriages have double roofs and both glass and venetian windows to protect passengers from sun-stroke on the journey.

The fares are;—first-class four and one-half cents, second-class, one and three-fourth cents, third-class, one-half cent per mile. This last is not expensive travelling. It would be equal to going through from New York to Chicago for $4.50, but, strange to say, this railway makes nearly all its profits, so far as passenger traffic is concerned, from its third-class passengers, at half a cent a mile. For the third-class carriages are almost always full, and often crowded, while as often the first and second-class are half or three-fourths empty, and sometimes a first-class carriage will go through a hundred miles entirely empty, or with but one passenger in it. Many trains run with one small first-class carriage, one second, and from eight to twelve third. The old saying on the continent used to be that "only lords, Americans, and fools travel first-class."

Here the higher English officials are obliged to travel first-class to keep up their dignity! A few wealthy natives nabobs also go that way to "cut a swell." The majority of foreigners, however, and Eurasians (half-castes) go in the more democratic second-class, and also a fair number of well-to-do natives, but they usually prefer to take a separate compartment from the Europeans. The multitude, consisting of the poorer Eurasians, and of Brahmins, Sudras and Pariahs, priests and people, artisans, traders, farmers, coolies, crowd into the cheaper and more popular third-class carriages. Being thus huddled together is a great leveller of old caste prejudices, and the railway thus becomes something of an educator of the people.

There is no means of communicating with the conductor, or "chief guard" as he is here called, while the train is in motion. Every fifty miles the train stops by a platform long enough for the "ticket inspectors" to come along by the windows and inspect the tickets of all the passengers, to see that none are travelling without tickets, and on alighting from a train you have to give up your ticket as you pass out of the gate. There is, however, in each compartment, placed conspicuously, a glass dial with an electric bell-push under the glass, and printed instructions attached to tell you that if any accident occurs to your car while the train is in motion you must "break the glass and press on the bell-push." This communicates with an electric bell on the locomotive, and the train is brought to a standstill, and the guard rushes along outside inquiring as to what has gone wrong!

At ten o'clock last evening I finished my sixty miles' journey with bullocks to the railway station, and awaited the incoming of this train. As it slowed up the chief guard sprang upon the station platform to see what passengers were to be accommodated. Finding me with a second-class ticket, and some twenty natives with third-class, he called to the under gaurd to crowd those into the already well-filled third-class carriages, and proceeded to unlock the door of a second-class compartment and assigned me a place on the upper shelf, the other "shelves" being already occupied. Spreading my small travelling mattress on the shelf, and placing my pillows and shawl thereon and my other small luggage at my feet, I climbed up and lay down. The guard shut and locked the door, and the train moved on.

At one o'clock we came to the junction of one of the chief branches of this road, where it took twenty minutes to make the necessary change of passengers and luggage, amid such a hubbub that a stranger to it would have thought that bedlam had broken loose. Hindus cannot accomplish much without double the noise of even Frenchmen. All of my fellow-passengers in this compartment left, and the train moved on with me as its sole occupant until about three o'clock, when we come to a large town where probably 100 passengers leave, and as many more get on.

The train stops here twenty minutes. Soon the door of my compartment is unlocked and opened by the under guard, and I hear a burly European voice arguing with him. I hear the guard, a native, saying to him in English, "No, I can't. See, there is a gentleman asleep in the upper berth." "Well, then, go and call the chief guard," is the response. I appear to be sound asleep and do not move. The chief guard, a native also, comes, peers in, and says, "No, I can't do it." "Well, then, I'll see the station master," is the reply. The station master, a portly native official, comes and looks in, (I am still apparently asleep) and says, "No, I can't disturb that gentleman after he has paid his fare and been assigned to his berth. It is contrary to our rules. You will have to put your wife and children in the ladies' compartment, right here in this same carriage, and yourself take a berth in here." After ten minutes more wrangling, to which I pay no attention, a rug is put in on the opposite lower seat, a portly form seems to lie down on it, and we move off. Every time we stop there are mutterings and imprecations on the guards, the station master, and the railway, but I appear to sleep on.

A little before sunrise, at a quarter to six here at this season, I appear to wake up, climb down from my exalted position, spread my mattress cushion on the lower seat, let down the upper shelves, take out my writing, and begin to pen further notes on my journey. But it is no use. My burly companion has been bottled up too long. He must talk or burst. I lay down my writing pad and pencil a moment to look in the railway guide, and out it comes; "Going far? if I may ask the question." "Only to the next junction on this train," is my reply. That is fifteen miles ahead. This express mail train runs just twenty miles an hour! So it will take us three-quarters of an hour to get there.

"Then do you take the other railway from there?" "I intend doing so." "As far as?" I smile and name the next junction, where I will have to change cars the second time. "Yes, glad to hear it. What do you suppose that humorous American, Artemus Ward, would have said to such a railway as this, and to these miserable carriages? Do you really suppose they are as good as those he characterised as 'second-hand coffins'? You have heard of Artemus Ward I presume?"

I admitted having heard of such a person. "Well," he says—and here he proceeded to quote that celebrated author's opinions on various questions connected with railway travelling; and suddenly brought up with "Your name, please?" I meekly give it. I have heard much of the world famed inquisitiveness of the Yankee traveller. I see at a glance that my companion is an Englishman, as proves to be the case, and I determine to humour him, and see how far he will go.

"My name is Jackson," he proceeds, "William Jackson, at your service. I hold such and such an office in the town this train stopped at, about three o'clock this morning. I've got a wife and five children with me on the train." I bowed my acknowledgments for this interesting piece of information, and my loquacious friend proceeded:

"This railway is a wretched concern, terribly mismanaged, with a fearfully inefficient staff of officials and employees. They demand high fares from their passengers, (he was paying one and three-fourth cents a mile) and yet they won't accommodate you a bit. Now I tried my best to get the station master and the guards to vacate this compartment when I got on the train, and let my wife and children and self have it to ourselves, but, bless you, they wouldn't do it. I kept at the station master the whole ten minutes the train was waiting, trying to make him clear it out and give it to us. (This meant, of course, turning me out bag, baggage, and bedding at three A. M.) but he was not accommodating a bit. Now on the —— Railway you can make the station master do anything you wish, but this fellow would not oblige us, but made my wife and children go into the ladies' compartment next (divided from this by a thin board partition) and put me in here alone, when I might have had my family with me all this time. It's too bad!" I assented that it was rather hard lines.

"Do you know Mr. So and So?" he resumed. I admit that I know them. "They are somewhat old friends of mine. You come from where?" With a scarcely suppressed grin I let him start on the catechism again, curious to see where he would run. His questions took a wide range and he pushed them with vigour. I found myself trying to recall my wife's maternal grandmother's maiden name, to be ready when that question should come, when a shriek from the locomotive announces our near approach to the junction, and gives me a great relief. Talk to me about inquisitive loquacious Yankee travellers after this! I never saw one that would come within shooting distance of this Englishman, though I confess such specimens are rare. So I suspect the "typical Yankee" specimens are.

Now the subject changes. He is also going to take the other railway here; but our train is twenty-five minutes behind time, and he is "perfectly sure we will miss our connection, you know, for the two companies are at loggerheads, and won't wait for one another at all; and what makes the matter worse is that to-day he is going on unusually important business,"—and he pauses for me to ask what that very important business is, but I do not take the hint. I have something more important to do. Through the open window I see that the train of the other road is waiting at its station, not ten rods from the one we are to stop at.

I get all my things ready, strap up my mattress, pillows and shawls, and the moment the train slows up, I motion with a coin in my hand to three cooly porters, toss out my luggage to them, which they seize, and follow me up over the bridge that goes over our train, and over the multitudinous tracks, and so on to the ticket office of the other road. I secure my ticket and get to the place for weighing luggage before any of our other passengers appear. On to the scales are piled my valise, bag, lunch box, mattress, umbrella, boots and pith hat! for everything must be weighed and extra paid for every pound in excess of sixty pounds, the limit of baggage allowed free to second-class passengers. I secure my receipt for that and the coolies bring my "belongings" on with me to the farthest forward second-class compartment, put the valise and bag and lunch box under the seat, receive their promised present, make their profound salaams, and run off to seek another job. I select the front compartment, for, if my catechetical friend *should* succeed in making the transfer with his family, I do not particularly desire that he should find me, and resume the domestic catechism, or talk me into a premature grave. I mop off the perspiration from my face, for the thermometer stands already between 90° and 100° in the shade at 6:30 A. M., and settle down for a thoroughly uncomfortable day, for I have to travel all day over some of the hottest plains of South India.

We are now on the narrow guage or metre guage line known as the "South India railway." The cars, or carriages, are much smaller; the locomotive much lighter and less powerful; the track not nearly so heavy, and the bridges of much cheaper construction, and as a consequence the speed at which trains are allowed to run is less, and the fare is less. An effort is being made to open out larger stretches of country with the same capital and the results are proving the wisdom of the experiment, but the traveller must be more patient, for it takes longer to run a hundred miles, and the comfort is less, for the train shakes and vibrates more.

About eleven o'clock we run into the Trichinopoly Junction, and here a half hour is given us for breakfast, for up to this time we have not had a chance to get anything to eat. We find a fairly good breakfast on the table, for the "guard" had telegraphed ahead the number of those who wished breakfast. In half an hour we are off on the other train which runs to Tuticorin, and this is perhaps the most arid, certainly the hottest part of our journey. In spite of the double roof of the cars, in spite of the double windows, to keep out the heat, the thermometer soon passes the hundred mark; at one P. M., it has passed 103° and goes on feeling its way toward 110°. No crops are on the parched fields except where irrigation allows rice to be grown, and that is very rarely on this arid stretch.

The native villages we pass by, with their streets of mud wall, thatch roof houses, look hot enough to burst out blazing from the sun's heat alone. When one house does take fire from any cause the whole village will be consumed in an hour. Many of the trees stand entirely without leaves, for the deciduous trees cast their leaves in the hot dry season instead of in winter, as in a cold climate.

By four P. M., we have reached the end of our railway journey at a station with a name as long as a whiplash, viz, Ammayanáyakanúr! Thirty rods from the station is a "Travellers' Bungalow" which is so much patronised that a butler is kept there, who supplies meals to travellers who telegraph him in advance, as I did. Thither I go with my belongings, and have time to wash up and rest a little before taking dinner at five P. M., for I do not wish to start on my "bullock transit" journey until the sun nears the horizon.

It is thirty-two miles hence to the foot of the ghát, or steep pathway up the mountain. A good road has been constructed by the government, and rival native companies have organised lines of transits, to take passengers through.

A bullock transit here consists of a two-wheeled cart with heavy wheels, with a box seven feet long and nearly a yard wide, over which is a woven bamboo cover. The body of the cart rests on stiff, unyielding springs attached to the axle, and in it is usually placed a bundle of fresh rice straw for the passenger, or passengers to lie on, and which the bullocks will eat at the end of the journey. The passenger puts his "resai," or light travelling mattress, or a rug over the loose straw, and getting in himself and lying down, with his luggage at his feet and side, he gives the word to be off. The driver springs onto his seat in front, with his bare feet hanging down so that he can with his toes grasp the tails of the bullocks and twist them to make them go, and off we start.

Being weary I was just falling into a doze when a rattling, whirring, metallic sound makes me spring up and look out; there in the dim light I see the tire of one of the wheels running off and tipping over into the ditch at the side of the road. A shout brings the driver to a halt, and in dismay he sees the mishap. An empty transit soon comes up, to my delight at first, but it proves to belong to the rival line, and with jeers and chuckles he drives on. The oxen are unhitched, and the cart left to stand until the driver goes to the town we had just passed, and, after a long time, appears with another transit, a very poor one, but in I get with my luggage and we are on our way again. Every six miles the bullocks are changed, and I strike a match, look at my watch, and, if the driver has made good time, give him a present, and tell the coming driver that he will have one if he drives well, and not without. Cat-naps are secured between, if the jolting is not too great, and at last the transit journey is ended.

At two A. M. we arrive at the tope, or grove at the foot of the ascent, and there, sleeping on the bare ground under the trees, in the moonlight, are the twelve coolies I had previously arranged for, for the ascent. Four of them are to take my luggage, and eight are to carry me up the twelve miles, climbing nearly 7,000 feet. One can ride up on a scraggy country pony, if he can endure it, or go up sitting upright in a chair, borne with poles, on the shoulders of six men, four at a time, and the other two changing with them. But as I am too ill and weak to sit up for so long, I have ordered a dooly, which is something like a short hammock hung to a long bamboo, and borne by two men in front, and two behind, the others coming along and changing every mile or half mile where very steep. If it is dark, a torch bearer goes in front, but there is a bright moon to-night.

The first five miles is up a valley by the side of a winding brook, and the ascent is very gentle, and good time is made. Then comes a mile of stiff climbing and the bearers put one down on the ground by a spring, announcing that they are going to have some breakfast. Often too they will slip away out of call and lie down and take a nap, leaving you with your hammock lying on the ground. But at last they return, and take you up, and after another half hour you come to the beginning of the famous zigzags up the face of the rocky mountain, which have been made at no small cost.

There are sixty-seven zigs, and sixty-seven zags, in this one place, and as the sun has now risen and is shining hot upon you the ascent is very wearisome. At their top another spring is reached, and another halt is made, and then, in four miles more of less steep climbing, with the sun pouring so hot upon one that he hardly realises that he has reached the cooler climate, you at last ascend the last zigzag to the eastern crest of the summit, and, passing under the shade of the trees, you are glad to put your overcoat on, as you dismount and look down upon the beautiful lake lying at 7,000 feet above the sea, and realise that you are in the climate of southern France in early summer, for the thermometer stands in the shade at 60° which is lower than you have seen it on the plains even in the coolest months, and you admit that a delicious climate and beautiful scenery and a grateful breeze reward you for your long, hot, wearisome sixty hours' journey.

XVII

A MISSIONARY SANITARIUM IN INDIA

KODAIKÁNAL is, perhaps, of all the sanitaria of India, the one most advantageous for, and the one most patronised by missionaries. It is about 7,200 feet above the sea, on the summit of the Palani, or Pulney Mountains, which separate the fertile Madura district of the Madras presidency from the native kingdom of Travancore. "The Pulneys," as they are called, are some forty miles long by twenty broad, and are a part of the mountain range, reaching from near Cape Comorin up to the north of Bombay, parallel with the sea of Arabia, and from twenty to sixty miles from its shore, and known in geographies as "The Western Ghâts." The Nilgiris and Mahâbléshwar are the more northern elevations of the same mountain range.

Half a century ago two of the missionaries of the Madura mission of the A. B. C. F. M., whose stations were near the base of these almost precipitous mountains, determined to accomplish their difficult ascent, to visit and preach to the

KODAI KÁNAL LAKE AND SANITARIUM

few mountaineers, and see what the climate might be, and whether it were not possible to have a sanitarium thus near them, in which to take refuge sometimes in the burning heat, or when ill, and thus avoid, perhaps, an absolute breakdown and an expensive journey to the home land for restoration.

Finding some of the hill people who had brought their wares to the periodical market at the mission station at the foot of the mountain, they induced them to pilot them, and carry for them a small amount of necessities up the difficult footpath utilised by the mountaineers. On reaching the summit they found a natural basin, whose bottom was about 6,900 feet above sea-level, with numerous springs of water bursting out of the sides of the hills that surrounded the basin, whose round and grassy summits were 7,300 to 7,700 feet above sea-level, and on whose sides were groves of forest trees.

Choosing a site in a grove 100 feet above the little brook, fed by all these pellucid springs, they erected a simple hut, with thatched roof and "wattle and daub" sides, and spent some days in it, testing the climate, exploring the hills, and preaching to the people they found in the few mountain hamlets. It were interesting to trace the experiences they had and their efforts to find a feasible coolie-path or bridle-road, up which coolies with loads, and ponies with riders, and donkeys with packs could come ; suffice it to say that ere many years had elapsed, by the aid of the district government officials, a passable coolie-ghat, and bridle-path, zigzagging up twelve miles from the foot, had been constructed, and a dam built, at small cost, across a narrow spot, turning the little brook into a beautiful lake, three miles around at the water's edge, into which fish were speedily introduced, and a few inexpensive houses had been erected by the Madras missionaries and the government officials of the district, who appreciated for themselves, and especially for their wives and children, the boon of having within a night's journey a change of temperature from 100° in the shade on the plain, to 60° or 66° by the little lake on the mountain.

This was the origin of the now well-known sanitarium of Kodaikanal. For many years its inaccessibility to all but those in the adjacent districts militated against its growth, for a journey of 350 miles by bullock bandy from Madras across the scorching plains to the foot of the mountains would prove too much for many an invalid, who might otherwise be saved and restored by its invigourating climate; and other sanitaria more readily accessible were patronised far more. Now, however, there is a railway from Madras to Tuticorin, near Cape Comorin, passing within thirty-two miles of the foot of the mountain, from which bandies (covered carts), drawn by relays of trotting bullocks, bring one by night, in from six to eight hours, to a little traveller's bungalow at the beginning of the ascent, whence starting before daylight one can come up in a chair or dooly borne by eight coolies, or can ride up on a scrubby country pony, making the twelve miles' climb, including the 100 zigzags, in five or six hours.

Houses, built of stone found in abundance on the spot in broken masses, as though already quarried, with red clay as mortar, have been erected among the trees on all the hillsides around the lake, and have been steadily creeping up from near the lake level until now the tops of the hills, 7,300 and 7,500 feet high, are utilised as building sites. The government astronomer kindly informs me that the government reckoning of the height of Kodaikanal is 7,209 feet above the sea-level, which I take to be the mean height of the residential portion of this mountain resort. The great Government Observatory for India now erecting is on a hill 7,700 feet high, overlooking the lake from the west.

It is singular that nearly all the great sanitaria of India, North and South, are at practically the same elevation above the sea: Simla being 7,116, Darjeeling 7,168, Ootacamund 7,271, Kodaikanal 7,209; while Mussúrie, Nynee Tál, Mahábléshwar, Coonoor, and the Shevaroys are a few hundred feet lower.

Kodaikanal has less non-missionary visitors than the other great sanitaria. Simla is the summer capital of the Viceroy, Darjeeling of Bengal, Nynee Tál of the Northwest Provinces, Mahábléshwar of Bombay, and Ootacamund of Madras, and hosts of government officials with their families accompany the governors there, and other Europeans swarm those places. In them all, and in others also, large and increasing numbers of missionaries too are found each season, obtaining a new lease of life for more vigorous work on the plains.

Kodaikanal, however, is a smaller and more quiet place. There is less of fashion; it is less expensive; it is more restful. Its climate is less damp than many of the hill stations. Being nearer the equator, in latitude 10° 15′ north, its climate varies but little in different seasons of the year. The thermometer 100 feet above the lake never goes below 40° in the cold months; it never rises above 76° in the hot months. In January and February frost is seen on the shores of the lake, but never 100 feet above. In April and May, the hottest months here, I have not seen the mercury above 75° nor below 60°, varying thus less than fifteen degrees night and day, week in and week out. Essentially the same as to the temperature during the hot months of the year, might be said of nearly all the great sanitaria of India. There is not the real tonic effect of frost upon the system. It does not build one up who is much run down, as a winter in the temperate zone does; but an occasional change to one of these sanitaria is exceedingly helpful in preventing the utter breakdown that has wrecked many a promising missionary career too near its beginning.

Missionary societies have come to appreciate the economy, both in health to the missionary and in money to their supporters, in having a sanitarium where their missionaries, jaded by months of incessant work in touring, preaching, school work, looking after the sick, working up more and more in the languages of the people, and, what so burdened the Apostle Paul, "the care of all the churches," could come for six or eight weeks of respite both from heat and from wearing work, and recuperate the worn physical and mental powers. It prolongs the years of service; it saves the lives of experienced missionaries, and prevents the necessity of so rapidly replacing them by novices. It forestalls the cost of many a long sea journey to the native land to save a life that would otherwise be sacrificed.

The "American Board," the leader in this wise movement, has been so convinced of this, that for more than thirty years it has provided a sufficient number of houses, inexpensive but comfortable, so that every member of their large Madura mission can find room here through April and May, the two most trying of the eight hot months of the year. These houses are then rented, as far as possible, during the remaining hot months, to others, usually the families of government and railway officials and European business men, and thus the expense of keeping up the houses is mostly met, and there is no drain on the contributions of the home churches for missionary purposes. Other missionary boards and societies are fast falling into line in affording these facilities, considering it in the interest of the truest economy so to do.

A Missionary Sanitarium

A missionary census of Kodaikanal, completed to-day, shows that there have come up so far, and are now in Kodaikanal, 170 missionaries, with sixty-two children, or 232 in all, of missionary families, representing fourteen different missionary societies, American, British, and German; in numbers the English being first and the Americans a close second; the Germans, Swedes, Australians, and Canadians being fewer.

It is not for a simple "play spell" that all these missionaries come up. Some indeed come so run down and ill that they must have absolute rest. Others come for change and recuperation with work, which they are able to bring up with them. The going over and valuing of hundreds of examination papers of the missionary colleges and schools whose spring term closes as their principals and teachers come up for the vacation, or the yearly examination papers of our native assistants who, each in his own village, carry on Biblical and theological studies through the year; the bringing up of arrears of correspondence and accounts; the preparation or revision of vernacular tracts and books; with young missionaries, the more vigorous study of the language; important committee work, that can be done better here than in the whirl of work below; these and other matters demand a good portion of the time of all who are able to work.

There is another most important advantage here to the isolated missionaries coming from scattered stations, who have little means of spiritual uplift through the year, except in private study and in the closet.

Every year there is held here, in May, a four days' convention for the deepening of spiritual life, to which we look forward with joy as one of the chief blessings of our sojourn. This year it was held May 7th to 10th inclusive, and was under the stimulating leadership of Dr. W. W. White, of Mr. Moody's Biblical Institute, Chicago, who has been giving two years of exceptional service to the young men of India. At each of our two daily sessions it was grand to see the earnest, joyous countenances of the missionaries that filled the American mission church, while we together considered the themes Christ, the Bible, the Holy Spirit, Prayer, and seemed to participate in the promised "fullness."

This week the annual Kodaikanal missionary conference meets for three days, for discussing important missionary problems, preparation for which has been made throughout the year. The sessions close with a united missionary breakfast in a grove, at which above 150 missionaries will be present and partake of food physical, and intellectual as well, in the after-breakfast speeches, and draw closer the bonds of missionary comity and loving friendship ere, next week, most of us go back to our more or less solitary stations, with new vows of consecration to Him who has given us so much of joy and uplift on these, His delectable mountains, for His glorious service.

XVIII

HOW THE "CUT" CUTS

YES. I think I can answer the question asked me as to "What Retrenchment Means in India," for I have recently met, in conference, missionaries of fourteen different societies and we have compared notes. We have told one another of our joys, yes, and of our sorrows and disappointments too, for on many of those missions the axe of retrenchment has fallen, fallen heavily, since from ten to thirty-three per cent. of the annual expenditure for work on the field has, in several instances, been cut off by the cut of retrenchment, and from the fullness of their hearts and mine I speak.

"Self-support among the mission churches" is, it is true, the apostolic plan, and none are working harder toward that end than the missionaries who are pushing the founding of native churches in India. To our joy steady progress is being made. In church after church in India a majority of the members give one-tenth of their income for church support and evangelistic effort.

Is that exceeded in happy, Christian America? But even that tenth makes but a small aggregate here, for the average income is so scant. "To the poor is the gospel preached," has always been the glory of Christianity. Even under the preaching of the apostles, "not many mighty, not many noble" were called. In India, too, God hath chosen the weak things of the world to confound the mighty. But the mighty are not yet confounded. It is still the weak. As yet those of our converts who have any property are, usually, in some way, stripped of it all, on embracing Jesus Christ as their Saviour. In few of our up-country congregations is the average total income of our members equal to seven dollars per month, while in hosts of our small village congregations the total income, per family, is not twenty-five dollars per year. And in these last three famine years often the village catechist, or pastor, himself on a salary of from three to six dollars per month for self and family, has had, out of that sum, to keep a pot of conjee, or gruel, boiling all the day, to deal out a little to the hungry or starving of his flock, or of inquirers.

What does retrenchment mean in India? I will give you a few composite photographs taken from those working in different missions, and from these safe general conclusions may be drawn, without a tedious array of statistics.

THE DISAPPOINTED HOPE

"Good news, wife, good news," called Mr. G., as he sprang from the horse on which he had ridden twenty-three miles from a trip in the district. "The people of three hamlets near Kôtur have given up their idols, pledged themselves to observe the Sabbath, and to obey all Christian teachings so fast as they are taught them. They promise to send their children to school to learn to read the Bible and Christian books, and I have promised to give them two teachers, for two of the hamlets are near each other, and one school will do for both. They are in hereditary servitude to the head man of the neighbouring caste town, and are wretchedly poor, but they seem to be really in earnest. We shall get hold of their children, even if we do not make very intelligent Christians out of the older people. Now if that extra $200 that I asked for in the new year's appropriation comes, it will just cover the absolutely necessary outlay in these three villages, and in the two that I received last month, eighteen miles south. There is evidently a movement toward Christianity among these down-trodden people, and if we can only provide them with teachers, we shall see a grand ingathering. Thank God for giving us this opening, for which we have long been praying and working."

His wife tried to look glad, but failed, as she led him in for the cup of tea and slice of toast she had prepared since seeing him come over the knoll a mile away, and until he had had this refreshment she would not tell him of the home mail, with its freight of crushing news that had come during his absence.

He needed the refreshment, for even then his hands trembled as he held the letter and read the imperative orders for a ten per cent. retrenchment on the last year's expenditure, instead of his hoped-for expansion, and then, putting his head on his hands, the strong man sobbed. "Then these seekers to whom I have promised the bread of life must go back and feed on their old ashes. O God, what does Thy Church mean thus to play fast and loose with thirsty souls?—to send me to proclaim in all this district 'Ho, every one that thirsteth, come ye to the waters,' and then strike the cup of the water of life from their lips as they bend to drink.

Merciful Jesus, show Thy Church what they are doing."

THE ABANDONED MISSION SCHOOL

The heart of Mr. K., missionary at Ténevúr, had been greatly gladdened two years before, by the reception of a petition from the town of Bíbinagar, twenty miles west, signed by the leading inhabitants, Brahmans, merchants, artisans, farmers, begging him to take under his charge, as a mission school, an Anglo-vernacular school which they had established a few years before for the education of their sons. They expressed their perfect willingness to have him introduce the Bible, as a text-book, in each class, every day, for they had noticed that the study of the Bible elevated the character of those who studied it, even though they did not become Christians.

He found these people in earnest. The fees paid by the boys entirely supplied the salaries of the present masters. The missionary put in better teachers and added a new Bible master. In two years the people had grown to appreciate the school so much that higher fees could be collected. But, with the Bible master, it still required $100 per year from mission funds to keep it up. It was worth it. Christianity was gaining its first foothold in that town, in that taluk, or county. The people were listening with respect, and attention, and interest, to the weekly preaching.

Then a heavy letter came from the Home Board; heavy with heartache. "Retrenchment, immediate, must be made at all the stations." The proportion falling on Ténevúr was Rs. 1,000 (three hundred dollars). Sadly Mr. K. went over every expenditure, cut off Rs. 50 here, 75 there, 100 in another place; dismissed three natives agents, though they knew of no other employment; and yet there was Rs. 300 (one hundred dollars) more that must be cut off. No other way could be found. The Bíbinagar school had to be given up. The Bible teacher was obliged to leave. It was reorganised as a heathen school, and Bíbinagar was enveloped in its pristine darkness.

THRUST BACK INTO HEATHENISM

"Jesus loves me, this I know, for the Bible tells me so," sang Sikâmani, (Crown-jewel), the little Brahman girl, as she entered her father's house from Miss v. R.'s caste girls' school in Singapúram, and her musical voice rang through the zenána apartments.

"Here, my lotus blossom, what is that you are singing? Who is Jesus? and what is the Bible?" asked her kindly-faced grandmother. "Come and sit down, and tell us all about it."

It was a leisure hour, and all the zenána women gathered and, seated on the mats around, listened while little "Crown-jewel" sang more of the beautiful songs Miss v. R. had taught them, in their own vernaculars. Then she told them all she had learned about that loving Jesus "who died that we all, yes, we women too, may be saved." Daily in this Brahman's home, in merchants' and artisans' homes, were such scenes witnessed since Miss v. R. had, one year before, opened the first Hindu girls' school in all that region. The school had filled its building in the Brahman street, and Miss v. R. had just engaged to rent another in the Goldsmiths' street, and open another school, and already scores of pupils had made application to be received.

Miss v. R. had come home joyously from completing the arrangements, making melody in her heart unto the Lord for giving her such opportunities, for she was already getting an entrance into one and another of her pupils' homes, to talk with their mothers and aunts. On her table lay the evening letters. One, from the secretary of the mission, she seized, opened, read, and sank into a chair, while disappointment and despair, too dry for tears, shook her slender frame. "Killing retrenchments ordered from home. No appropriation for Hindu girls' school. Must close them all from end of next month." That school cost Rs. 225, or $75 per year. The new one would cost the same. But the home church was too poor to afford the $150, so the order had come as to all those Hindu homes into which the light was beginning to steal, "Shut out the light, shut in the darkness."

DR. ANNA AND HER PATIENTS

Dr. Anna B., sent out five years before, had opened out a very fine and desperately needed medical work in Bilanagar. Her hospital with twenty beds for in-patients was always filled, while the hundred out-patients daily were blessed with her medicines, her skill, and her prayers. The seeds of the kingdom were daily sown in hundreds of grateful souls. Some seemed germinating. More patients were begging for treatment than she could possibly receive on her appropriations. She had sent a strong appeal for an increase in funds, and an assistant or associate, as the work was more than she could do. "Impossible. Funds not coming in. Cannot keep up even present appropriations. Retrench fifteen per cent. from January 1st. Imperative."

Sick at heart she went over every expenditure to see where she could possibly cut down. Medicines and necessaries for treatment must be had. A small reduction was possible in a few minor points, but on "diets of in-patients" must nearly the whole reduction fall. There was no help for it. Hereafter but ten of the twenty beds could be filled, for the people coming from distant villages were all too poor to provide food for themselves away from home. Ten beds were packed away, as they were vacated. The remaining ten were all filled with important cases, and Dr. Anna prayed for a hard heart, to enable her to refuse others.

"Will the dear lady doctor please come and see a dying woman in Kullúr, four miles north?" A young mother, fourteen years old, whom native midwives had horribly maltreated, from want of skill and knowledge, was what she found. Her life might still be saved by the utmost skill and care, if she could be placed in a hospital, not otherwise. "Bring her in on her bed. I will try." Half-way back and Dr. Anna was stopped at a hamlet to see a young girl, terribly gored by a bull. "Bring her in too." As she neared the hospital a woman wrapped in a blanket tied as a hammock to a long bamboo, and "borne of four," was laid on the veranda of the hospital, with a foot dropping off from gangrene, the result of the bite of a poisonous, but not deadly, serpent. The love of Jesus pulsed in Dr. Anna's heart. She could not say no. "Take her in," and so of two others equally needy who came. But how were they to be fed?

Dr. Anna had already devoted all she could spare from her small salary to purchase additional medicines for the growing throngs of outpatients. Now, to feed these, her suffering sisters while they were being healed, she gave up the more expensive articles in her own diet, meat, eggs, fruit, etc., and struggled on, giving her every energy to her increasing number of patients, and working harder, if possible, even on her unnourishing diet. Months thus sped by. One morning she fainted at her work, and fell upon the masonry floor of her hospital. An adjacent missionary was hastily called. An English doctor of experience and skill came from the large town near. "Nervous prostration and threatening paralysis, from overstrain and lack of nourishment. Must be put on the first steamer and sent home as the only hope," was his unhesitating verdict.

Her Board had saved $100 by the cut, and paid $200 to take home poor wrecked Dr. Anna B. The sick were deserted, and the hospital closed. The murmur went around the home land, "What a mysterious Providence that strong and vigorous Dr. Anna B. should be stricken down after only six years of service, and just when she was most needed."

* * * * * *

These incidents occurred in no one mission, in no one year. But they are true illustrations of what are the terrible burdens put upon her missionaries by the wholesale cuts ordered by the home church, in ignorance, let us hope, of the havoc they sometimes necessitate. Only a few of the actual workings of retrenchment have been pictured, for my heart is too heavy to gaze further myself, or open to the gaze of others all that a ten, twenty or thirty per cent. reduction involves. For here and there, in this mission and that, it means all that I have pictured, and more.

Retrenchment means the dismissing of faithful

catechists in half-instructed little village congregations of those too poor and hungry themselves to feed the catechist and his family. It means the sending away of Bible women, and zenána workers who are gaining an entrance, or are eagerly welcomed in many houses where "the Sweetest Name" is beginning to be lisped. It means the closing of scores of day-schools attended by the worshippers of Vishnu or followers of Mohammed, who, in those schools, are daily reading and learning the teachings of the Nazarene. It means the giving up of preaching tours in "the regions beyond," with glad invitations to the gospel feast. It means the closing or cutting down of schools for training young men and young women to be the Timothys, and the Loises, yes, the Barnabases and Pauls of the militant church of Christ in India. It means the sending out word to all seeking communities who are too poor to pay for a teacher. "Don't give up your idols and avow yourselves Christians now, for we can send no one to teach you how to find and follow Jesus!"

O Christ, who seest Thy crippled work, Thy delayed chariot in India, rouse, rouse Thy people to a just appreciation of what they themselves owe to Thee; of what Thou dost expect of them.

Summon with insistent, with resistless voice, those redeemed by Thee to become Thy working-partners in that stupendous work, the salvation of a sin-lost world.

XIX

HOW HINDU CHRISTIANS GIVE[1]

THERE are a few peculiar facts in connection with the work carried on by your missionaries in India which the Church at home should know. There has hitherto been a misunderstanding in the matter. It is time that it was corrected. The matter that I refer to is the benevolence of our native churches in India.

I have been asked by ministers of our church within the past few weeks,

"Why is it that the native churches in India do so little in the way of benevolence and self-support? Do not the last minutes of the General Synod report the whole contributions of the churches of the Classis, or Presbytery, of Arcot for these purposes to be only $996.00?"

Upon my replying that they are not backward in their benevolence *in proportion to their means,* the further question was asked,

"Do no men of means join you among your converts?"

[1] An address before the General Synod of the Reformed (Dutch) Church at New Brunswick, N. J., June 7, 1886.

It is to the peculiar facts connected with the solution of the first of these questions that I now ask your attention. The second will be answered later on.

The difference in the real value of money in India and America is the first of these facts.

I hold before you two coins. The one is a silver dollar, the other is a dime. You notice the difference in size, you know the difference in value. You will doubtless be surprised when I tell you that in purchasing power of food, of clothing, and of labour among the natives, the dime in India is worth fully as much as, if not more than, the dollar in America, and this fact must be taken into account in estimating the real benevolence of the native churches. But first let me explain the facts.

I said that the dime in India is worth as much as the dollar in America in procuring the food, clothing, and labour of natives. To prevent misunderstanding I must, however, here premise that it is not so as regards the necessaries of life for Europeans. It has been proved by experiments, costly in life and health, that Europeans cannot live in India as natives do. They cannot live in native houses, dress in native clothing, and live on native food without loss of life, or of health. We must, if we would retain vigour for successful work, live somewhat in the style, and have somewhat of the comforts, to which we have been accustomed at home. But the moment that we step outside of the native diet, articles of food become expensive. Our clothing, or materials for it, must all be brought out from England, France or America, and on it we must pay freight, duty and commission. So of books, periodicals, newspapers, and all the numberless little necessaries and comforts of life. Thus, alas, to your missionaries in India the dollar is worth, in very many things, much less than the dollar at home.

But among natives it is different. The equivalent of a dime counts more in wages in India than the dollar in America. In Arcot, Vellore, and Chittoor, the best bricklayers, the best masons, the best carpenters can be hired for twenty-five cents a day. Will multiplying by ten secure you the labour of masons and carpenters here? Harvest hands will work all day in India for from six to nine cents, and board themselves. You must multiply by twenty to secure hands for your harvest fields in America. The cooly women will work all day in the fields or in the house for from three to five cents per day. I pay my gardener and water-carrier $2.75 per month, and he boards himself, and that is considered good wages. I can hire a man with oxen and cart for $7.50 per month, and he boards himself and feeds his oxen. The teachers of many of our village schools receive a salary of but $30 to $36 per year, to support themselves and family. Our highest paid native pastors receive but $150 salary. Not more than two receive that. The most of our native preachers or catechists receive from $60 to $90 per year.

So much for wages. The cost of living is in proportion. I remember a fairly educated single man, who had recently come to Madanapalle for employment, appealing to me in trouble, saying that they asked exorbitantly for board there, and that he could not stay. I asked him how much he had to pay. He told me, with great indignation, that they had the face to charge him $1.75 per month for his board, and that he had never paid so high in his life before!

As for clothing; a fairly well-to-do man's suit, complete, will cost from $2 to $3, and a woman's from $1.75 to $2.50. Rich men and women dress extravagantly there as here. Our native preachers make their pastoral calls and preach in suits costing not over $3 to $4. The wedding trousseau of the bride of a native preacher usually costs not more than from $10 to $14. A student can be educated in the Arcot Academy or the Female Seminary for from $30 to $40 per year, according to age, and that includes board, clothing, books, tuition and incidentals. Many a father would be glad to have his son's expenses here come within ten times that amount.

You will see at once that the income and the expenditure of our native Christians in India must be multiplied by ten to approximate at all to income and expenditure among our churches in America. You must apply the same rule to their benevolence, when comparing it with the benevolence of our home churches. If in this light you will look at the statistical tables in the last minutes of General Synod, you will see that the benevolent contributions of the churches in the Arcot Mission are not small.

The Classis of Arcot is young, and not yet strong. Let us compare its contributions with some of the country Classes of the Church at home. For this purpose I have taken one Classis from the Synod of New York, one from the Synod of Albany, one from the Synod of Chicago, and one from the Synod of New Brunswick. Each of these Classes is older than the Classis of

Arcot. The four Classes I have chosen (one from each Synod) aggregate 6,857 communicants, and their contributions for "Religious and Benevolent Purposes" (not for the support of their own ministry), as given in the table, aggregate $5,-309.87, or 77½ cents per member, on the average.

In the same table you will see it stated that the Classis of Arcot, with its 1,582 members, gave for the same purposes $511, which is equal to 32⅓ cents per member, or if you multiply by ten, as is only fair from the above showing, you will find that their real benevolence is equivalent to $3.23 per member, or more than four times that of the American Classes just mentioned.

But in order that we may understand what the native benevolence really is, and what self-denial it requires, let us take a single church in the Classis of Arcot, and analyse its benevolence, and the resources of its members. For this purpose I take the church of Madanapalle, because I know its benevolence, and the circumstances of its members better than I do those of any other church in the Classis of Arcot. That you may verify my statements, I take the report of the Board of Foreign Missions for this last year, 1885–6, which has just been laid before Synod, and which is now in your hands. In the statistical table of the Arcot Mission you will find it stated that the Church of Madanapalle, with its seventy-four communicants, contributed for all purposes Rs. 275. The rupee is worth just a half-dollar in silver, and for all purposes of comparison, both in expenditure and income, I have reckoned two rupees to the dollar. Thus calculated, the contributions of the native church of Madanapalle for 1885 would be $132.50 for the seventy-four communicants.

Now, who are these seventy-four members, and what are their circumstances? I know them well. The average income of fifty-five of them would not be over $30 per year. That of ten others is over $48 and under $60. That of eight others is over $60 and not over $100. Only one member of that church has an income of over $100, and his is $162. The total yearly income of these seventy-four members would then be:

55 averaging	. . .	$ 30 =	$1,650.00
10 "	. . . .	54 =	540.00
8 "	. . . .	72 =	576.00
1	. . . .	162 =	162.00
Total yearly income	. .		$2,928.00

Divide this total yearly income among the seventy-four church members, and you will have the average yearly income of $39.57 per member, and yet they give for benevolent and church purposes $1.85 per member, or nearly one-twentieth of the total income of the members.

Can you show me one single church in our whole communion in America that gives one-hundredth of the income of its members for benevolent and church purposes? If you can, I will go directly to that church and present the missionary cause, assured of a rousing collection.

In the Board's Report, it is stated by Dr. William Scudder, the resident missionary, that the Madanapalle church has been employing and paying the salary of Abraham Nannia Sahib,—the convert from Mohammedanism,—in evangelistic work among the Hindus and Mohammedans of the "region beyond." He is the missionary of that church, solely supported by them.

Out of the total contributions of Rs. 275 spoken of above, this little church, only lately gathered in a heathen land, pays to the Pastors' Fund the equivalent of one-half of the salary of the Senior Catechist (the unordained native preacher in charge of the church), and supports its own missionary among the heathen beyond, and over and above this, contributes out of their poverty $1.08 per member to outside benevolence.

How Hindu Christians Give

In the minutes of Synod before referred to, it is shown that the 83,702 members of the Reformed Church gave last year $233,996.46 for "Religious and Benevolent Purposes," aside from the support of their own churches. This makes an average of $2.80 per communicant for the whole Reformed Church. By the side of this, place the $1.08 per member actually given for outside benevolence by the church at Madanapalle, and then multiply it by ten, as shown above, to find their real comparative benevolence, and you will have your Hindu Christians giving the equivalent of $10.80 per member, per year, as against the $2.80 per member of the church in America.

Will my friend who asked the question a few weeks ago ask again: "Why is it that the native churches in India do so little in the way of benevolence and self-support?"

Does not the Classis of Arcot, tried by the above standard, the rather stand out as the Banner Classis of our whole communion? I have spoken only of the church at Madanapalle, but the church at Tindivanam and other churches in our mission would make nearly the same showing had we the data to work them up.

How is this amount raised among these comparatively moneyless people? Our Christians give until they feel it. The senior catechist at Madanapalle, who has been supported for twenty-three years by the Sabbath-school of the church in Kinderhook, N. Y., and who receives only $100 salary, always gives in benevolence one-tenth, and often one-eighth of his income, as I well know. He has a family of eight children. One of the higher paid native pastors in our mission, who receives nearly $150 per year salary, makes one-tenth his minimum, and often gives one-eighth or one-seventh of his income to the Lord.

Scores of our native Christians loyally make one-tenth their minimum in giving, and those who have no money give in substance. In many of our Christian families in the villages who have no money to give, the mother, with the consent of the family, takes out a handful of the allotted grain as she prepares the daily meal, and when Sunday comes makes the family offering unto the Lord in kind.

The pupils of some of our boarding-schools agree to go without a part of the scanty portion of meat that is allowed them only on certain days of the week, and jointly contribute the price of the meat saved in the collection on Sunday. In other of our schools, when the rice is taken out for the midday meal by the cook, one of the pupils goes, by appointment of the others, and takes out so many gills of the rice and puts it into the treasury basket, and on Saturday it is sold and the avails divided around to be put in the collection on the morrow.

At a missionary meeting at which I was present, as we were raising missionary money, one member said: "I have no money that I can give, but I have a new milch cow; I will spare one-third of all the milk she gives until she goes dry, if any one will agree to take it daily, and put the value in money in the missionary collection." The milk was at once bespoken, and that cow gave milk well and long that year. A widow woman took off her choicest "toe-ring" (for they use them there as much as finger rings), and put it in the contribution box. It was purchased for half a dollar, and that sum went into the box as the widow's gift.

And other widows give until we sometimes hesitate to take all that they bring to consecrate to the Lord. Our native Christians are not all liberal. There are some in India as well as in America who seem to wish to get everything from Christ and give nothing to Him. But your missionaries strive, both by precept and by example, to teach them the blessedness of giving for the Lord's work until they feel it. I know of no missionary who does not consecrate at least one-tenth of his small income to the Lord, and we try to bring all our converts up to the same standard; and of very many in our churches we can joyfully say, as did Paul of the churches in Macedonia, "For to their power, I bear record; yea, and beyond their power they are willing of themselves; for their deep poverty abounded unto the riches of their liberality."

When this matter is fairly understood the Hindu native churches will no longer be chided for the meagreness of their contributions.

XX

A MERCHANT OF MEANS JOINS US

THE second question asked by my interrogator as mentioned in the last chapter was, "Do no men of means join you? How is it that your native churches in India are financially so weak?"

Yes, some men of substance have joined us, but their substance has not. In every case where men of position and property have become Christians in our mission, they have suffered the loss of all things. I could give a number of instances to illustrate this. I will give but one and that briefly.

Bála Chetti, a merchant of Palmanér, was converted in 1865, under Dr. Silas Scudder, then the missionary there. An account of the conversion is given in the annual report of the mission for that year. Bála Chetti was a well-to-do merchant of the town, of high caste and extensive family connections. He was one of several brothers who held an undivided ancestral estate, and carried on their business in common. He had been an inquirer for some months.

He finally broke his caste and became a Christian. A mob collected, armed with various weapons, seeking to kill him. He eluded them and escaped to the mission premises. On Sunday, when he went to church with the missionary to be baptised, the carriage in which they went had to be guarded by the police. The church was surrounded and taken possession of by the mob. Only He who restraineth the wrath of man could, and He did restrain that mob. Bála Chetti took refuge, for a time, at the mission house. When the excitement was somewhat over, he went to his house in the town. His wife had, before this, when he first became a Christian, spat upon him, and gone home to her parents, taking their only son with her.

He now found that his brothers had walled up with masonry the entrance to his part of the large common residence. He could only get in by climbing over the barred scullery gate in the rear. He found it deserted and empty. He wished to continue with his brothers in the management of their bazaar. They spat upon him in the streets, and would not let "this dog of a Christian" enter their place of business. Foiled in this, he brought suit in the Civil Court for the division of the paternal estate, that he might take his share and do business alone, if they would not allow him to keep on with them.

His brothers brought in forged documents and suborned witnesses to swear that he had already drawn out and squandered the whole of his share of the estate. Not a witness could be found to testify for this "renegade and outcast." They dared not. The judge openly said he suspected the documents to be forged and the witnesses false, but there was no rebutting testimony, and the case went against him, and his property, that might have been a help to the Christian church, was all gone.

After a time he brought suit in court for the recovery of his wife. She was summoned and appeared at the District Court presided over by an English judge. She was asked if she would return to him? "No."

Had he not been a kind husband? "Yes."

Had he ever abused her or neglected to provide for her and their son? "Never."

Why would she not return to him then? "Go with that Christian dog! Never!"

Did he not love her and did she not love him? "Yes, before he became a renegade to his ancestral faith; but now he was dead, so far as she was concerned."

He lost his wife and child and brothers and house and lands and property for Christ's sake and the gospel's. All was gone but his faith in Christ, but to that he held firm.

He remained for a time with the missionary, studying the Bible. He could not again be a merchant. He had been boycotted; nobody would buy of him, and besides his capital was all gone. To gain a livelihood he enlisted in the government police, under a Christian officer. That he might be free from continual insults and persecutions he was sent to a distant district. The cholera swept throught that district, and Bâla Chetti was taken up. His old friends said, "What a wreck!" They little knew his eternal reward.

From this one representative case you will see how it is that the Church of Christ in newly-entered districts in India is still poor; why our churches must still be helped. But the leaven is working. It is working among the higher classes as well as among the low. The time is coming, it draws near, when multitudes from all classes and castes will join us, and bring their substance with them. Till then let the Church of Christ in Christian countries throw in her help in no stinted measure, and, by the aid of God's spirit, the enginery will be produced that will roll through India and carry it all for Christ.

> "I gave My life for thee,
>   My precious blood I shed
> That thou might'st ransomed be,
>   And quickened from the dead.
> I gave My life for thee,
>   What hast thou giv'n for Me?"

XXI

"BREAK COCOANUTS OVER THE WHEELS"

WE had recently located in the heathen town of Madanapalle, India, to commence missionary work there. The time for the annual drawing of the great idol car through the streets of the town and by the banks of the river had come. Multitudes of votaries from all the villages around, as well as from every street of the town had assembled before the car. Great rope cables were attached. Hundreds caught hold of the ropes. Up went the shout, "Hari! Hari! Háyi! Jayam!" "Vishnu! Vishnu! Joy and Victory!" "Now *pull*," shouted the priests, and off went the three-storied car majestically through the streets, amid the joyous shouts of the thousands of spectators. On they followed it to the river bank. Libations were brought and poured over the car, and the multitudinous ceremonies performed.

Again, with similar shouts, they began the progress around by different streets, back to the great temple before which the car always reposed

HINDU POTTERS AT THEIR WORK

A GROUP OF HINDUS AT DINNER

for the year. Half-way back and the car came to a stand.

"Pull," shouted the priests. Pull they did. The ropes snapped with the strain. All the wheels were examined; no stones were in the way; everything seemed right. The ropes were tied and new ones added. More votaries caught the ropes. "All pull," shouted the priests. All bent to the effort. It would not move.

A pallor came over the crowd. "The god is angry and will not let his chariot move," was whispered along the streets. A feeling of dread shivered through the multitude. "Yes," shouted the Chief Priest from the car, "the god is angry. He will not move unless you propitiate him. Run all of you and bring cocoanuts and break over the wheels, and as the fragrant cocoanut milk runs down over the wheels the god will accept the libation and graciously allow his chariot to move on again. Run, and each bring a cocoanut. Run!"

Men and boys ran for the cocoanuts; the residents to their houses, the villagers to the bazaars to buy, or to their friends' houses to borrow. Each came back with his cocoanut, and broke it over one of the wheels. The cocoanut milk ran along the streets.

"Háyi! Jayam," shouted the priests. "The god is now propitious." "Háyi! Jayam!" "Joy! Victory!" shouted the multitude. "*Now*, PULL ALL," shouted the priests. The people took heart; dread passed away; confidence came. They seized the ropes and, with a shout that resounded in the hills a mile away, they gave a pull. Off went the car, and soon, with singing and dancing, they had it back in its wonted place. And as the crowd scattered to their village homes, the news ran through the country: "The car got set; they could not move it a finger-breadth; but each man brought a cocoanut and broke over the wheels, and then on it went with a rush to the temple."

I could not help recalling this incident the other night as I read the important Financial Statement laid by the Secretary of the Foreign Board before the recent missionary convention.

God's chariot is delayed. His Chariot of Salvation had started in its course in towns of India and China and Japan through the agency of the Reformed Church. Have the people lost heart, that it stands still? Has discouragement come upon us?

"*Run for the cocoanuts.*" Let each man and boy, let each woman and each child bring what would be to them the equivalent in value of a cocoanut to the poor Hindu, as an offering to the Lord, and the chariot will move joyously on.

Had one rich Hindu given a thousand cocoanuts to break over the wheels of the idol car, and the multitude not given any, the effect would not have been at all the same. Each one of the throng made an offering. Each one felt that he had a share in it. Each one took courage. Each one shouted. Each one pulled and on went the car.

The missionary chariot halts. Many villages are pleading for a missionary or a native preacher. Young men and women, eight of them, are offering to go out to the different missions. Heathen schools are offered to the missionary to introduce the Bible in. Young converts ask to be trained to be preachers to their kindred. Every mail tells our Board of onward steps that should be taken. The Board cannot reply, "Go on," for debt stares them grimly in the face.

Shall this continue so? Dare we let the Lord's chariot halt? Oh, that every one of the 80,000 members of the Reformed Church, every one of the 90,000 children enrolled in our Sunday schools, every one of the 200,000 adherents, who enjoy the weekly ministrations of our sanctuaries here in this gospel land, would hasten to bring in an offering if not more than the value of a cocoanut, and then with a heart in the work they would unitedly send up a pæan of praise and a shout of Joy and Victory, and God would be pleased and His chariot would move on right gloriously.

In one respect our illustration fails; for here the well-to-do disciple may give his hundreds and the rich his thousands, and, they will help on as only hundreds and thousands can.

Here it is not a limited number of cocoanuts that can be used. It is not *one* chariot that is delayed. The wheels are set in Tokyo and Yokohama and Nagasaki; in Amoy and Sio-ke; in Tindivanam and Chittoor and Madanapalle; and new chariots should be put in motion in other places. Let the well-to-do send in their cocoanuts in cooly loads and cart loads, and elephant loads, aye and ship loads, for there is need of all. Let each one, man, woman and child, bring in his offering even as God has prospered him, and bring it with the gladsome shout of one alive to his privilege and expecting victory.

Our harvests have been plentiful. Let us put God to the proof. "Bring ye all the tithes into the storehouse, and prove me now herewith, saith the Lord of Hosts, if I will not open the windows of heaven and pour you out a blessing that there shall not be room enough to receive it."

Let the cocoanuts come. Who brings the first? What church sends one for every man, woman and child on its roll? Who sends the cooly load? Who the elephant load? Who the ship load? "Please answer soon."

XXII

THE WEAVING OF INDIA RUGS, OR GOD'S PLAN IN OUR LIVES[1]

In complying with the request of the Classis of New Brunswick that I should be the one to give the charge to you to-day, I find so many memories crowding upon me, so many conflicting emotions filling my mind, so many joyous anticipations taking possession of my soul, that I find it difficult to choose fitting words with which to fulfill the pleasing duty that is laid upon me.

For memory takes me back at a single step over the intervening space, as I so vividly recall the scene when, just twenty-seven years ago, my much loved Hebrew preceptor, since then your venerated College President,[2] gave similar words of counsel when he preached the sermon at my ordination as a missionary to India, and joined then in laying hands of consecration on my head, as he has now done on yours.

[1] The charge at the ordination of William I. Chamberlain as missionary to India, in Rutgers College Chapel, June 20, 1886.

[2] Rev. William H. Campbell, D. D., LL. D.

The Weaving of India Rugs

Twenty-seven years of blessed service for the Master! How packed with labours and with joys! For, in looking back over these years of missionary service, it is not the hardships and trials, but the blessings and joys that fill my vision, and to this blessed heritage of service for the Master do I now bid you welcome with unfeigned gladness.

And what should be the spirit with which you enter upon this life service for Christ in India? What should be your highest aspiration? What shall give you your surest success, your supremest joy in that work?

I desire to place before you in this solemn hour as at once your highest aim and your most potent weapon, "*Personal Conformity to the Image of Christ.*"

Paul in the eighth chapter of Romans, declares that we are called of God "to be conformed to the image of His Son," and he speaks of this as a growing conformity, as in the third chapter of Second Corinthians, where he says, "We are changed into the same image from glory to glory." And the beloved John tells us what shall be the consummation, when he says in his First Epistle, third chapter, "When He shall appear *we shall be like Him.*"

This becoming conformed to the image of Christ is a gradual process. The change begins with regeneration. That is indeed instantaneous. It is then that the *germ* of conformity to the image of Christ is implanted, but unless it grows it remains but a germ. Regeneration is instantaneous. Sanctification is progressive. And as we grow in the grace and in the knowledge of our Lord and Saviour Jesus Christ we grow into conformity to His image.

For this growth in conformity to His image the continual aid of the Holy Spirit is absolutely necessary, but it also requires *persistent and earnest personal effort* on the part of the believer, and to such effort after personal conformity to the image of Christ, would I now seek to incite you more and more, as you enter upon your life of service for Him.

Such growth into Christ's pattern is not easy work. It is not, with most of us, an uninterrupted growth. There is sometimes even retrogression, and we become disheartened, and think we can never attain, and are almost ready to give up trying.

I have thought of this struggle to imitate the Divine pattern as I have stood watching the slow weaving of those beautiful *India rugs* which, when completed, are so much sought after and so highly prized.

India rugs are all the product of painstaking, long continued hand labour, requiring closest watchfulness at every step, lest the figure be not perfect. I have often stood watching the workmen and thinking of God's plan in our lives.

The rug, however large it be, is woven in one piece. The warp is stretched vertically upon the simple loom. There is no shuttle. There is no beam. The weaver sits or stands facing the perpendicular warp. The only light in the room is from a window behind the weaver, shining over his shoulders full upon the growing rug before him. With deft fingers he runs in the different coloured woolen yarns into the warp in front of him, and, with a heavy wooden comb, combs it down to its place, and with hand-shears clips off the too long protruding yarn. As you stand behind his back, and at one side out of his light, watching him, he goes on, apparently forgetful of your presence, chanting to himself from memory the pattern he is weaving in as he swiftly inserts the threads, "six black, three brown, five red, seven white," and so on, as the hours go by. Now and then, as he completes a figure, or part of one, he steps back to take a look and see if it is perfect; but, alas, he has made a slip.

Some inches down, where he has not been giving due heed, his pattern is marred. Heaving a sigh, he again takes his place, and laboriously takes out the last half hour's, or last half day's work, and more carefully builds it over, for it must be perfect or it will not be accepted.

I have looked in one day and the rug seemed progressing finely, but the next there seemed to have been absolutely retrogression, so much had been taken out to remedy a just discovered defect; but it goes on to final completion.

I have myself seen one rug six months upon the same loom, and the weavers had been working upon it day by day, and all day long. Orders were on hand that would take them two full years to fill, but the process could not be hurried, or defects were sure to creep in.

Sometimes, as you looked in, you would see something out of harmony; you could not tell what it was, but felt that something was wrong. The weaver, too, had discovered it; he carefully studies his pattern, finds where he has gone wrong, toilsomely remedies the defect, and as you step in again, the want of harmony has disappeared, and the perfect figure greets your gratified view.

May not this be taken as an illustration of *God's pattern being interwoven into our lives?*

The pattern is glorious; is perfect. But in weaving it into our lives what sad mistakes we sometimes make; how much we have to undo of what we have carelessly done. How often we find something that is out of harmony with God's plan, and yet the peculiar defect of which at first eludes our search. But as we study more closely the Divine image we see at last, by the illuminating influence of the Holy Spirit, where the defect is, and heaving a sigh and seeking more light from over our shoulders, we at last weave in the pattern as God intended it. And at length, under the guiding eye of the Master Workman, our life pattern is "complete in Him."

French imitations of these India rugs are now thrown on the market by the hundred. They are machine woven. The patterns are indeed exact. There is no distortion in any figure, but it is machine perfection. The rugs cannot compare in richness and life with the laboriously handmade rugs of India, and no one who knows the true India rug will fail to note the difference, and though produced at one-fourth the cost, and sold for one-fourth the price, the demand is still for the more expensive handmade genuine India rugs.

There is no machinery for producing God's pattern in our lives, for producing "conformity to the image of His Son." It is a slow, laborious hand-work, to be done by each believer as he watchfully follows the Divine guidance in his life. But when this is accomplished how glorious the result, for "when He shall appear we shall be like Him."

Let this, then, be your highest aim, your daily study, your hourly effort, as you enter upon your chosen life's work, and as you join hands with your Jesus in the completion of the work for which He gave His life—even the salvation of the whole race of man, *imitate your Master*. Do day by day as He would have you do; as He would do in your circumstances, and the result in your own life pattern, and in the conversion of those for whom you labour, will be glorious.

Waste no time in vain regrets over past failures, or newly discovered faults in the weaving of your life pattern; but in humility asking God's free pardon for the errors of the past, say with the Apostle Paul, "This one thing I do. Forgetting those things which are behind, and reaching forth unto those things that are before, I press toward the mark for the prize of the high calling of God in Christ Jesus."

To-day there has sprung up a new relationship between us. For nearly twenty-four years have we been related as father and son. Now I gladly welcome you as a brother-minister of the Lord Jesus Christ. The natural tie can never lessen; but let the new spiritual tie grow stronger and more all-controlling, as the Master allows us to be *comrades* in His glorious war, and *brother-ministers* of the New Covenant in that distant land, where, God willing, our lives are to be together offered to Him who has bought us with His own precious blood.

Yet bear with me while I reiterate to you the words which Paul the aged used as he exhorted his younger brother in the ministry, his son in the faith, Timothy, when he said:

"Thou, therefore, my son, be strong in the grace that is in Christ Jesus." "Endure hardness, as a good soldier of Jesus Christ." "Watch thou in all things. Endure afflictions. Do the work of an Evangelist. Make full proof of thy ministry."

For then will you be able to join in Paul's triumphant shout of victory: "I have fought a good fight. I have finished my course. I have kept the faith. Henceforth there is laid up for me a crown of righteousness which the

Lord, the righteous judge, shall give me at that day."

My son, my brother, I welcome you to the glorious fellowship of the missionary of the Cross of Christ Jesus, our Lord.

XXIII

"DESPONDENT MISSIONARIES"

An hour ago the overland mail came in. I took up one of our Home Religious Periodicals, one that is usually well informed on all missionary matters, and that is thoroughly sympathetic with missions and with missionaries. In an article on the very first page, it makes use of the expression, "Our faithful, but now desponding missionaries abroad."

I laid down the paper, wiped my glasses, and looked again, to see if I could have read it right. Yes, there it was, "desponding missionaries." Where are they? Perhaps there are such, but I do not know them. Yes, there must be, for there it stands in that well informed Periodical. Again I laid down the paper and began to think and question, Where are those "despondent missionaries"?

I have not seen them. But then I have not had much chance. It is only four and a half months since I came back to India, after a somewhat prolonged absence in America, and things may have changed; I must make inquiries.

I saw a number of missionaries in Bombay, to be sure, when I landed, but my time was short, and they had only time to tell me of victories recently won; of new campaigns on which they were just entering for further conquests, and their faces were radiant, not despondent, as they spoke. But perhaps I misjudged them.

On the second afternoon of our railway journey from Bombay to Madras, at a junction we were joined by a large party of missionaries just going to their annual meeting. They had closed the work of the year, tabulated their gains, written their reports. Seven of them were old personal friends, whom I had known as fellow-fighters for from fifteen to twenty-seven years. If they were despondent, they concealed it well. For two hours we had a compartment to ourselves, as they told me of victories scored, and obstacles overcome, since we last met, and of the grand openings for further fighting in the coming year.

Just one week from that day I was in council with the missionaries of the Reformed Church of America, at our annual meeting at Vellore. Tales of more organised opposition, of increasing obstacles I did hear, but not of yielding to the opposition, nor of succumbing to the obstacles. The whole thought seemed to be, how shall we best organise our forces so as not only to hold our own but make larger conquests in the year to come.

And when, a few weeks later, we and our native brethren gathered at Palmanér to inaugurate our new Theological College, for the Endowment of which I had been able to secure during my last six months in America, gifts aggregating nearly sixty thousand dollars, that we might be able the more thoroughly to train a more earnest, better equipped body of soldiers for the deepening conflict, the jubilant shouts of joy, thanksgiving, hope and courage for this new leverage for more aggressive warfare, could not have been mistaken by even the most bilious dyspeptic, for moans of despondency. It was rather the "Marseillaise" of the coming liberation in the name of Christ.

From there by previous invitation, I went to Madras to meet the "Madras Missionary Conference" composed of some seventy missionaries of all societies, English, Irish, Scotch, Germans, Danes, Americans, Hindus, to tell them of the proposed movement on the part of the Y. M. C. A.'s of America for organising a work for the millions of young Hindus who know not God. I was at their preliminary business meeting.

There was no whining over defeat, but vigorous plans for further assault. I was with them through the hour of social intercourse, and the sparkling eye and earnest utterance, as one after another told me of contests and campaigns and battles and victories while I had been away, had not the flavour of despondency. Nor did the wrapt attention, and frequently manifested approval during my forty minutes' address on "Our God Given Opportunity now in India, and How to Turn it to Victory," by organising an army of young men to work with and for young men, with Young Men's Christian Association methods, nor the enthusiastic speeches that followed mine, indicate a despondent frame of mind.

It was one of the most enthusiastic meetings I have attended in India, and enthusiasm is not born of despondency. The greatness of the obstacles now before us was clearly recognised; the marshalling of the enemy's forces as never before; the new forms of more vigorous opposition; the crisis now upon us; each was distinctly seen, but "By God's help we will win the victory," seemed the prevalent thought in each mind.

"Despondent missionaries!" Well, yes, we might possibly be despondent if we had time to sit and think and brood over the fewness of the recruits, and the smallness of the supplies, and the leanness of the Home Treasuries. But we have no time for that. If the recruits be few, we must each be up and do the more. If the supplies of funds be inadequate we must try the harder to make $10 do the work of $20. We have no time to look down. We have to look up, and we see God the Father, God the Son and God the Holy Ghost, all pledged for, and working for the victory; and the victory will come.

No! I have not found the "despondent missionary." If there be one I would be glad to hear from him. I should like to know him, and to ask him why he desponds. And besides, a well-marked exception always strengthens the rule.

But with deep solicitude we missionaries do look upon our loved churches at home, and a dread comes over us sometimes, when we think of the many in the home churches who do nothing to help forward this mighty battle for victory, and we almost fear that the Divine fiat may go forth, with reference to some of them, "For if thou altogether holdest thy peace at this time, then shall there enlargement and deliverance arise from another place; but thou and thy father's house shall be destroyed; and who knoweth whether thou art come to the kingdom for such a time as this."

XXIV

THE CHANGE OF FRONT IN INDIA

A GENERATION has fully passed since the writer, in 1859, joined the ranks of those attempting the conquest of India for Christ. How different the condition and the outlook then and now! Then India was just emerging from the troublous and turbulent times of the great Sepoy Rebellion. The sway of the East India Company, which had been growing, for some two centuries, had recently been merged into the rule of Great Britain's queen, and religious toleration had been proclaimed throughout her dominions. Then the first 200 miles of railway had just been opened; now some 20,000 miles run through all the provinces. Then western education was in its infancy; now 15,000,000 of the educated classes all through the land, but chiefly in the large cities, freely use the English language, and are more or less well up in western science and western thought, the vernaculars, however, still retaining undisputed sway in the households of all.

Then Hinduism was as firmly seated on its throne as it had been at any time since the days

UNDER TRAINING FOR A "DANCING GIRL"

AN INDIA ALOE PLANT IN BLOOM

of Moses. It had, indeed, passed through a slow process of modification, of deterioration. The essential monotheism of the Védas of Moses' age had degenerated into the polytheism of the Shástras and Puránas, and farther, into the gross forms of idolatry of the later period, with its 330,000,000 of deities, named and unnamed. The system of caste, invented long after the Védic period, and gradually imposed upon the people, binding them hand and foot, and preventing all genuine progress, still manifested all its power, and one would sooner die than break caste rules, and lose his caste and so his soul.

Then Hindus thoroughly believed and upheld and practiced their religion. Then Benares, Tirupati, Sri Rangam, Raméshwaram, and the host of holy places were monthly thronged with their scores of thousands, and in their yearly festivals, by their hundred thousand pilgrims, and on all the roadways you would meet the returning pilgrims with two brass pots hanging from their *kávadi*, or neck-yoke, filled with holy water at the Ganges, and replenished at each of the sacred streams as they wearily walked their thousands of miles to their distant homes. Then they believed in the efficacy of these pilgrimages and penances and tortures.

In February, 1861, I met a venerable Brahman pilgrim who told me of his sixty years of pilgrimages—of twice ten thousand miles—to every sacred shrine in India, all made on foot, and begging his food by the way. "And yet," said he sadly and with disappointment—"and yet, the burden of sin is just as heavy as when a young man, I started on this quest. Oh, sir, does your Véda tell how I can get rid of this burden of sin, and be at peace with God?" One sees no such pilgrims now.

Then hook-swinging and spike-walking and self-torture and immolation were real verities. Yearly the shrine of Juggernaut saw its throngs of 100,000 devotees, from hundreds or thousands of miles of toilsome pilgrimage, and thousands gripped the long cables dragging the ponderous car of Juggernaut, while devotees were throwing themselves beneath its wheels.

Now, all is changed. Britain's sway, indeed, has put a stop to torture and immolation, but the waning faith of the people in their religion has been putting a more effective quietus to the ancient order of things, until recently Juggernaut's priests issued the dismal wail that not enough pilgrims came to pull the car around its annual outing, and scarce were they able, with all the coolies they could hire, to move it back to its home.

The throngs of devout worshippers, making toilsome journeys, with costly gifts, have ceased. Lessening multitudes now go, indeed, but by train, with more or less comfort, to many of the shrines, and perfunctorily engage in some of the less irksome ceremonies, but little or none of the religious spirit is seen.

Then the rich endowments of the temples were yearly increased by the liberal gifts of those who believed they could thus buy release from sin. Now myriads of temples are slowly going to ruin, and a wail comes up from the priests of the most noted shrines at the smallness of the offerings, while the people are openly accusing the priests of squandering in voluptuous licentiousness the revenues from the endowments of the pious dead.

But let us note Hindu testimony on this point.

One hundred of the chief residents of Tirupati, the most noted shrine of southern India, signed and sent a memorial to the Viceroy of India, in May, 1894, calling his attention to the desperate condition of Hindu religious endowments in general and of those of Tirupati in particular:

and praying that government would provide more efficient means of safeguarding the interests of such endowments.

The *Daily Hindu*, one of the strongest native papers in India, the organ of all the orthodox Hindus of Madras, published the memorial and thus commented upon it:

"We may well feel shocked at the true yet wondrous tales of huge frauds and heinous crimes which the memorialists have catalogued. The glory has departed out of our religious institutions, and what once contributed to purify the minds of millions of men and women are now the grovelling ground of some of the most ignorant and wretched of human beings,—who merely wallow in a mire of voluptuous pastimes, wasting the pious contributions of the widow and orphan, and breeding around them a whole host of idle, able-bodied vagabonds. The vast majority of these endowments are corrupt to the core. They are a festering mass of crime and vice and gigantic swindling."

What a change of front since the leaders of Hindu thought were the ardent supporters and rich benefactors of these very temples!

The *Reis and Rayyet*, an influential Calcutta orthodox Hindu paper, sneers at Mrs. Besant's ecstasies over the beauties of Hinduism, and justly says:

"When an English lady of decent culture, professes to be an admirer of Tantric mysticism and Krishna worship, it behoves every well-wisher of the country to tell her plainly that sensible men do not want her eloquence for gilding what is rotten. . . .

"If the *Upanishads*, (Commentaries on the Védas, etc.,) have a charm for Mrs. Besant, she is quite welcome to proclaim her views on the subject. But the *Upanishads* do not form any part of the religion of the Hindus as it is found in their everyday life. In actual practice they are either Sivites or Saktas or Krishna worshippers. In fact, abomination worship is the main ingredient of modern Hinduism, and we therefore ask Mrs. Besant to study the subject a little more carefully than she yet appears to have done. If she will follow our advice, she may, provided she is sincere herself, sooner or later, admit that the course she is now pursuing is fraught with mischief."

Of the Brahmanic priesthood in India at the present day, *The Hindu*, the representative native newspaper, before referred to, speaks in these scorching words:

"Profoundly ignorant as a class, and infinitely selfish, it is the mainstay of every unholy, immoral and cruel custom and superstition in our midst, from the wretched dancing girl, who insults the deity by her existence, to the pining child-widow, whose every tear, and every hair of whose head shall stand up against every one of us who tolerate it, on the Day of Judgment. Of such a priestly class our women are the ignorant tools and dupes."

It seems now to be the profound conviction of all thoughtful Hindus that Hinduism as it now exists, as it was when Christian missions began their campaign in India, as it has been for the last two thousand years, must go.

The stanch, orthodox Brahman editor of a vernacular newspaper is quoted by *The Missionary*, London, as taking this gloomy view of the situation:

"We entertain no more any hope for that religion which we consider dearer than our life. Hinduism is now on its deathbed and unfortunately there is no drug which can safely be administered to it for its recovery. There are native Christians nowadays who have declared a terrible crusade against the entire fabric of Hinduism, and many men of splendid education are also coming forth, even from our own community, [Brahmans] who have already expressed a desire to accept Christianity, and should these gentlemen really become first Christians and then its preachers, they will give the last deathblow to Mother Hinduism. This terrible crusade is now carried on by Christians with a tenacity of purpose and devotion which in themselves defy failure."

But while all thoughtful Hindus seem to agree that Hinduism, in its modern form at least, must go, they are not by any means agreed as to what shall take its place. All agree in fighting aggressive Christianity. They have even borrowed Christian tactics and have formed, in many cities of India, "Hindu Tract and Preaching Societies," and are issuing millions of pages of tracts, attacking Christianity, and scattering them broadcast. Some of them are of a most blasphemous character, and filled with grossest falsehood. Others are simply designed to arouse Hindus to a sense of their danger. One of these, as translated from Tamil by Dr. J. W. Scudder, makes use of the following language, a singular admission for enemies to make:

"How many thousands of thousands have these missionaries turned to Christianity! On how many more have they cast their nets! If we sleep, as heretofore, in a short time they will turn all to Christianity without exception, and our temples will be changed into churches. Is there no learned Pandit to be secured for money who will crush the Christians?

"Do you not know that the number of Christians is increasing, and the number of Hindu religionists decreasing every day? How long will water remain in a reservoir which continually lets out but receives none in? Let all the people join as one man to banish Christianity from our land."

There are three distinct trends of thought on the part of those who unitedly oppose aggressive Christianity.

One party seeks to resuscitate Védic Hinduism; to purge modern Hinduism of all its undesirable later accretions, and restore it to its pristine purity. But no two agree as to what its "Undesirable accretions" are, nor as to what the "Pristine purity" should consist in. Some say it must be monotheistic, and without caste distinctions. Others wish to retain a few of the more popular gods, and to keep up caste distinctions. There seems at present no prospect of an agreement as to what this "Revival of

Hinduism" should consist in, though there are multitudes of preachers of such a revival. What will be the outcome of this no one can say.

The second trend is toward the acceptance of a Christianity without Christ,—that is, the accepting of Christ's teachings as a system of morality, without accepting the name of Christians, and without admitting Christ to be Divine.

The *Indian Social Reformer*, edited by non-Christian Hindus, in a notice of the American Arcot Mission's report for 1894, makes this evident, as in the following extract:

"Why does not Christianity progress? The situation at present admits the report, is 'unpleasant and disheartening,' to the missionary. Why? The reason to our minds is this; the ordinary missionary attaches more value to the name than to the spirit of Christ, and judges of his labours by the number of his [avowed] converts. The true Christian spirit, which is also the true spirit of all faith, *is* making way. Is it so very difficult for our missionary friends to see that the mind which revolts from the dogmas and extravagances of Hinduism will not accept those of Christianity? That the man who rejects the theory of the incarnation of Ráma would not believe in that of Christ? No, no. Emancipation is once for all.

A godlike man is still a man and not God. There is our difference with our Christian brother in a nutshell.

"We concede that Christ is one of the most perfect, the noblest of men. We read the Bible and listen awe-struck to the Sermon on the Mount, and pass on to the soul-stirring sacrifice on Calvary. Does it move us one whit less—this immortal heroism—that we believe that the hero was a man? And why do you want more?"

A few would go still further in their admission, and, in their willingness to borrow from Christianity, even professing to believe in the incarnation of Christ, but, with the same breath, declaring that they believe Buddha and Zoroaster to be incarnations of the deity.

The Amrita Bazaar Patrika, a stubbornly orthodox Hindu newspaper of North India, in an editorial has these words:

"There is scarcely an educated man in India who has not read the Bible. It is impossible for a Hindu not to feel a profound respect for the Bible. The real fact is that every true Hindu is a believer in Christ also. There is not a true Hindu all over India who does no believe in the *Avatar*, [Incarnation] of Christ. Indeed, in the matter of devotion to Christ, the Hindus and

Christians are on a perfectly equal level. There cannot be the least objection on the part of a Hindu to pray, 'Save me, Father, for the sake of Jesus Christ.'"

They would simply add Christ, with His inimitable life and teachings to their pantheon, but remain Hindus or non-Christians all the same. To this end, "The Arjya Literary Society in Calcutta, composed of non-Christian Bengali gentlemen" we are told, "are now engaged in translating the Bible into classical Bengali. They have asked and obtained the assistance of representative men of the Christian communities, lest anything should appear in the translation which should make it anti-Christian in tone."

The third distinct trend is toward agnosticism; and this I regard as the most portentous trend of all, for it exists not only among those who openly so avow themselves, but untold numbers who, for social reasons, ally themselves with some one of the other parties, have really thrown themselves into blank and cheerless agnosticism, and the number is increasing faster than we know.

There is, however, in spite of all the above mentioned opposition, an unquestionable undercurrent tending toward evangelical Christianity.

There came to me secretly in my tent, when out upon a tour, a native gentleman high in office, in caste, in social position, of whom I have spoken at length in preceding chapters, wishing to have a private conversation with me on the claims of Jesus of Nazareth to be the Saviour of the world. After a somewhat extended conversation he said to me, in substance:

"Sir, I am not a Christian. I am still regarded as a devout Hindu. I still perform enough Hindu ceremonies to avoid suspicion, but in my heart I dare not deny the claims of the Bible. I *see the power of Jesus Christ in the lives of His followers so distinctly that I cannot deny His Divinity*. He must be Divine or He could not work such a change in the lives of those who become His disciples. He is not yet my Saviour. Caste, wealth, position, family all hold me back; but even now I never allow Him to be spoken against in my presence. I have long been reading the Bible in secret. The more I read of Christ and ponder over His life and teachings, and the power to conquer sin, which comes from embracing His religion, the more do I feel that in the end I shall have to accept Him at any cost, as my personal Saviour; but how can I do it now and bring ruin upon my family?"

There are more such than we have any idea of. The surface currents so often fail to tell what the deep-sea movements are.

Sir Charles Elliott, Lieutenant-Governor of Bengal, for thirty years a close observer of missionary activities and missionary problems in many provinces in India, said in a public address:

"There is unquestionably an undercurrent working among the higher classes in India toward Christianity, in spite of all the open manifestations against it, and we may look forward with confident expectation to the day when all India shall bow at the feet of Christ, who alone can uplift, purify and save."

This changed front, then gives royal vantage ground to work for India's redemption. The old apathy; the supercilious indifference; the old silent, but dogged resistance; the old conviction that naught could shake Hinduism's firm foundations, has passed away, and passed never to return. Religious thought in India is drifting hither and yon. The time to rally all Christ's forces has come. Let earnestness of effort and persistence in prayer bring out and energise these secret half-disciples. The currents that are veering away from Christianity may now, by

God's blessing on trebled effort, be turned toward the Cross of Calvary, and India yet be won in this generation. The time for work is now.

XXV

VERNACULAR PREACHING: IS IT INEFFECTIVE?

An extract from Dr. Norman Macleod's "Address on Missions in India," as given in the appendix to his memoirs, has been forwarded to me by a distinguished divine, noted for his earnest interest in foreign missions, asking that I would give my opinion "as to his claim that the mere proclamation of the gospel to the adult Hindus is ineffectual,"—that is, stated boldly, that vernacular preaching alone, without previous education in Western science and culture, is ineffectual for their conversion.

There is much that is just in Dr. Macleod's characterisation, in that address, of the theological terms in common use in the vernaculars of India, as containing misconceptions. But we must remember that Dr. Macleod's visit to India, made a quarter of a century ago, was chiefly to his own missions; to those holding the Scotch educational ideas, and who gave themselves almost entirely to educational work in English, and who did not know the vernaculars well, if at all, their work being in English. He imbibed the idea that you must first educate the Hindus and then convert them. His address contains a strong and keen presentation of their side of the question.

On the other hand, the published "Fundamental Principles" of the Arcot Mission of which I am a member declare the other view, to which we more and more firmly adhere, viz :

"We believe that India with its teeming population is accessible to the preaching of the gospel from her lowliest village to her most crowded city. We believe that God has endowed the Hindus with an intellect peculiarly capable of comprehending the truths which He has revealed, and with a conscience fitted to be awakened thereby.

"We believe that the vernacular languages of India furnish media fully adapted for the clear and forcible communication of divine truth.

"We believe that Christ's commission, recorded by the Evangelists, enjoins as the definite plan of missionary labour the promulgation among the population of the gospel in their own tongues ; the perseverance in the use of the means until individuals and communities are proselyted to the Christian faith, and the teaching of proselytes and their children ;" and, therefore,

"That each missionary, as far as possible, should make the preaching of the gospel to the heathen in the vernaculars his chief work."

On these principles the Arcot Mission has carried on its main work from its establishment. Of the 7,513 converts it is safe to say that more than ninety per cent. have been brought in by this "public proclamation" of the gospel. Admittedly a large proportion of these is from the lower classes. But of our converts from the higher castes it is also true that a large percentage has been brought in by this "public proclamation" of the gospel in the vernaculars. John Silas, the Arni Brahman, converted and baptised in our mission in 1862, and who died an efficient native minister in an adjoining mission, never attended a mission school or an English school a day before his conversion. He heard the proclamation of the gospel by our missionary at Arni, in the streets, repeatedly. He obtained Tamil Gospels and read them, and was converted and nearly lost his life because he came out boldly and embraced Christianity. Abraham William, the converted Reddi, the beloved and successful native pastor in our mission, owed his conversion to street preaching in Chittoor. Isaac Henry, the lamented Bible teacher in the schools of Vellore, was brought to Christ by the vernacular preaching in the mission hospital at Arcot, where he was a patient. John Jacob Ráyappa, the Brahman convert at Madanapalle in 1891, was brought in solely by village preaching and tracts. Old Seth Reddi, the father of the beloved John Hill and Samuel Seth, the head man of his village, and whom I buried in Palmanér in 1861, was brought in by the reading of tracts and gospels in Telugu, and so with a majority of our Brahmans and other high caste Hindu converts too numerous to name.

The different meanings they have been accustomed to associate with the vernacular theological terms we have to use, such as sin, salvation, regeneration, heaven, etc., does indeed constitute a difficulty. Paul had exactly the same difficulty to contend with when he went forth among the idolatrous Gentiles, when he discussed with the polished Greeks of Athens and Corinth. But, in spite of that difficulty, he was successful in introducing Christianity in those lands by the use of their vernacular, steeped in idolatry and false ideas though it was. So will we be, if we judiciously use and explain the vernacular terms they have, and earnestly, lovingly, and with faith push the work. Some of the incidents given in my sermon on "The Bible Tested, or How the Bible Works in India," published by the American Bible Society, show distinctly that Hindus do comprehend and are sometimes moved by our public proclamation, and that they have a conscience for sin which is capable of being aroused by this oral proclamation.

Dr. Macleod says: "In no case, moreover, will the educated and influential classes listen to such preaching."

I join issue with Dr. Macleod. He has never tested it. I have. I have stood for two hours in the public streets of a city with the streets packed with the Brahmans, merchants and city elders, keenly discussing the claims and the doctrines of Christianity, and their astute and wily objections thrown in showed that they were comprehending and fearing the power of the truth. I have had such audiences in the Mysore kingdom and the Hyderabad dominions, as well as in British India. After a long discussion in the market place of a Mysore city with the chief priest of the place surrounded by seventy of his pupils, and the educated people of the city, and which had been carried on into the darkness of the night, closing with the promise of the priest to meet us there in discussion again the next evening, that very priest came secretly to our tent, in a grove near the city walls, the next day, at midday when all the people were in their houses at their meals, so that no one should see him come, and, after an interesting conversation, making sure that no one else heard him, he made to us this frank confession:

"Sirs, what you said yesterday in the market place was utterly unanswerable. I did the best I could to defend my own position, surrounded as I was by my own disciples, but I am not going to meet you in discussion again. What you said is so pure, so holy, so good, it so appeals to the highest desires and needs of men that it seems as though it must be true; it must be divine. At all events it is a nobler religion than ours. But, sirs, we Brahmans cannot afford to let you succeed. We are now treated as demigods by the people; we reap the rich revenues from all these temples; at every festival we receive rich gifts; we are looked up to and worshipped. But let your system succeed, which teaches that there need be no human mediator, no mediator between God and man but Jesus Christ, and we Brahmans drop from our high pedestal down to the level of common men, and must struggle with the ignoble throng for an existence. No, sirs, your system is better than ours. It is so pure, so holy, so good, it appeals so to the highest desires of the human soul that it seems as though it must be divine. But, sirs, we Brahmans cannot afford to let you succeed in introducing your religion. We have got to fight you."

That statement, so unusually frank, may furnish a key to the often repeated assertion, "We don't know what all this means. It is so foreign, so Occidental that we do not at all comprehend it." It is not that they cannot understand God's plan of salvation even when presented in the vernacular and with defective theological terms which we must explain and illustrate as we use them, for this Brahman priest knew no English, and had never before met a missionary, and yet he took its essentials all in. It is that the natural heart there, as everywhere, abetted in the case of the Brahmans by powerful self-interest, stands out stoutly against the truth, and none the less with those who have received an education in Western lore. The very few conversions from among those educated in mission colleges, in the quarter century since Dr. Macleod made that address, do not warrant us in delaying the proclamation of the gospel until India's two hundred and eighty millions have been educated in Western culture.

Higher education has its place in the uplifting of India, and a noble place it is. It is a grand auxiliary power, and in our mission we use it as such. But to say that without it as a forerunner the peoples of India cannot comprehend the way of salvation through Jesus Christ, cannot understandingly accept of Him as their Saviour, is a reflection on Him who gave the command, "Go, preach the gospel," and who said, "he that believeth and is baptised shall be saved."

We of the Arcot Mission press forward in this vernacular proclamation of the gospel, foolish though it seem to some, in the absolute confidence that the incoming fruits will fully sustain Paul's declaration that "it pleased God by the foolishness of preaching to save them that believe."

XXVI

A UNIQUE MISSIONARY MEETING ON THE HIMÁLAYAS

SIR CHARLES ELLIOTT, the Governor of Bengal, and Lady Elliott last week sent out cards of invitation for a reception to all the missionaries of all societies now working on these hills, numbering more than eighty, including those working at Darjeeling, Ghúm, and Kalimpóng, and those visiting this sanitarium for recuperation.

The principal residents of Darjeeling, and tea planters on the slopes of the mountains, and many officials up here, on duty with the governor, or on leave, were also invited by Lady Elliott to meet the missionaries.

Sir Charles has had long experience in India, rising from the bottom of the Civil Service ladder, up through the different grades, by sheer force of character, until he has attained by appointment of the Queen Empress, to his present exalted position. In government official parlance he is styled the Lieutenant-Governor of Bengal, because the Governor-General, or Viceroy, also has his headquarters in Bengal, and of course, overshadows him. But Sir Charles is, *de facto*, Bengal's governor, having his own Legislative Council, and his own Cabinet, or Secretaries, entirely distinct from those of the Viceroy.

Darjeeling is the Summer Capital of Bengal, and during the hottest months Sir Charles and Lady Elliott occupy "The Shrubbery," as the gubernatorial residence here is called, with its beautiful garden-park around it, and government offices and chief officials adjacent; and from here the affairs of the great Bengal Presidency are, for the time, administered.

The cards of invitation read "To a Garden Party at 4:00 o'clock, to be followed by a Drawing Room, at which an account will be given of the Progress of Missionary Work."

A break had come in the Monsoon weather now upon us, and the clear day with the view of eighty miles of snowy mountains added to the zest with which all parties came together. The Governor and Lady Elliott were exceedingly affable, having pleasant words of cheer for each missionary, as they enquired after their work, and taking special pains to introduce the missionaries and officials, residents, and tea planters, who were present. After an hour's very pleasant social intercourse, during which refreshments were served to all, Sir Charles passed through the company, inviting all to come to the "Durbar Room" or Reception Hall used on State Occasions, and the company was quickly seated on sofas, divans and chairs placed in an unconventional manner all around the spacious room.

Pleasant conversation ran on for a few minutes, when order was called, and the Governor, stepping to a table at the head of the room, gave a brief address of welcome, which was so pleasant and so telling that I have written it out briefly, that others too may enjoy it and be helped and stimulated by it.

Sir Charles spoke substantially as follows:

"Missionary friends, Ladies and Gentlemen: I wish in a few words to say what a very great pleasure it gives Lady Elliott and myself to welcome so many missionaries here as our chief guests this evening, coming as they do from all parts of our Presidency as well as from the other Presidencies and Provinces of India, and representing so many different missionary societies, from so many different countries.

"We are very glad that so many missionaries can come up to this delightful climate, from the burning plains, for a little well-earned rest and recuperation, after their soul absorbing and arduous toil at their stations, for it will fit them the better for the heavy work ever before them.

"It gives us real pleasure to tender to them this small amount of hospitality, with a large amount of sympathy and good will, and of appreciation of the noble, and to India, all important service that they are rendering.

"*My long experience in India, in the different Presidencies and Provinces has taught me that the British Government in India cannot possibly do the work which, in the Providence of God, is our only justification for being here, namely the civilisation, enlightenment, and uplifting of the whole people of India, without the aid of the missionaries.* For extended observation, and careful study of the people, have produced in me the profound conviction that nothing can lift these millions of Hindus up to the standard of our Western Christian nations in probity, morality and nobleness of life, but that gospel of Christ which has lifted us up.

"I view, then, the missionary work as an *indispensable, unofficial, voluntary auxiliary of the government* in carrying out in India its highest aspirations, the ennobling of the whole Hindu people. Always in our tours in the provinces Lady Elliott and myself find our greatest pleasure in looking up and trying to help and encourage the missionary work of all societies wherever we go. We are grateful to you missionaries for your self-sacrificing labours and for the help you thus render the government, and I assure you, that you will always find sympathy both in 'The Shrubbery' where we now are, and in 'Belvidere' House in Calcutta, so long as we continue to occupy it.

"I wish further to say, that Lady Elliott and myself have to-day invited you, the leading residents and visitors at Darjeeling, and tea planters of the district, that you may meet these missionaries, and learn of their work and learn to know them personally, and so henceforth take a much greater interest in their work, and render them the more liberal help. If they give their lives to the work, it is only fair that we should aid in furnishing them abundant supplies.

"I congratulate you all that the last census, and the signs of the times all point to a very positive and somewhat rapid progress of the missionary work in India. There is unquestionably an undercurrent working among the higher classes in India toward Christianity, in spite of all the open manifestations against it, and we may look forward with confident expectation to the day when all India shall bow at the feet of Christ, who alone can uplift, purify and save."

At the nomination of the governor, Bishop Johnson, the Anglican Bishop of Calcutta, and Metropolitan of India, then took the chair, and, in a brief address, thanking Sir Charles for his outspoken testimony to the missionary work, and him and Lady Elliott for the kind conception and kind action which had assembled this company, went on to say that his duties as Metropolitan of India, taking him from the Himâlayas to Cape Comorin, and from Karáchi, on the sea of Arabia, to Assam, on the borders of China, gave him the opportunity of guaging any progress made in the missionary work, not alone of the Church of England, but, to some extent, of all other societies within those wide limits; that when he first came to India, a decade ago, he did not, at once, appreciate the amount of preparatory work that had been done, not to be tabulated in any statistics, not apparent to the eye of the casual observer, but which he now saw to be the chief element of hope for the speedy evangelisation of India. He told of the numbers of educated native gentlemen who, to his knowledge, were now privately reading the Bible, and endeavouring to conform their lives to its precepts, while still outwardly adhering to Hinduism, who ere long, when the Spirit of God should mightily move among them, would come over, as a mighty host, into the Christian Church. He spoke of the wonderful uplifting power which Christianity had already manifested in the Madras Presidency, in those regions where very large numbers of converts had been gathered, and referred to the remarkable declaration of the Director of Public Instruction in Madras in his last official report on the progress of education, to the effect that if the percentage of increase during the last twenty years be maintained, the native Christian population of that presidency would within the next two generations have surpassed the Brahman in education, in intelligence, in material prosperity and in official position. He intimated that he had come to India interested, indeed, in missions, but practically a pessimist as to their progress; that a decade of close observation had converted him into an optimist, for the well-marked indications now were that India would, in the not very distant future, become an integral part of the Kingdom of Christ.

Rev. Archibald Turnbull, B. D., the senior missionary, in the Darjeeling District, of the Church of Scotland, to which seems to be committed the evangelisation of the Eastern Himálayas, gave a terse and interesting account of the work going on among these Hill-people, with their twelve catechists and twenty junior assistants, at Darjeeling, and at twelve out-stations, reaching to the base of the mountains; Nipáli Catechists for the Nipális who have immigrated in such numbers from the adjacent Kingdom of Nipál, in connection with the tea industry; Lepcha Cathechists for the Lepchas from Sikkim, and a Bhutía Catechist working among the Bhutías, who have flocked in from Bhután; and told of the little churches they had already established here with 1,700 adherents, and 600 communicants, with baptisms of new converts every month. He also spoke of the Scotch Ladies' Zenána Mission in Darjeeling, consisting of three Scotch ladies, and one native woman, who carry on their work in and around Darjeeling in four languages,—Nipáli, Hindi, Bengali and Hindustani.

Miss Edith Highton, of the English Church Zenána Mission in Calcutta, followed with an intensely interesting account of their methods of work, their hindrances and their successes.

Rev. Mr. Gwynn, of the Church Missionary Society, in charge of their Training Institution in Calcutta, then told of his work, and instanced remarkable cases of conversion of young men of the higher classes from their study of the Bible in mission schools, who had, indeed, lost all, of property and friends, but had gained Christ; thus effectually answering the oft repeated taunt that Hindus only become Christians for worldly gain.

Rev. J. A. Graham, M. A., of the "Young Men's Guild Mission" of the Church of Scotland at Kalimpóng, in British Bhután, spoke of the exceedingly hopeful work in his mission, with 200 baptisms of mountaineers last year, and of the native Church organising a "Foreign Missionary Society" among themselves, to send the gospel into the Kingdom of Bhután adjacent, into which no European can yet enter; and of the resignation from mission service of the senior and highest paid native evangelist, who had begun the work at Kalimpóng, some twelve years ago, that he might go forth as the first foreign missionary of the native church to the turbulent and dangerous regions of Bhután, receiving only the voluntary contributions of the native Christians to support him in Bhután, and his family in Kalimpóng, since they could not accompany him.

He also spoke for the "Scottish Universities' Mission," in Independent Sikkim, now under the efficient charge of Rev. Robert Kilgour, B. D., of Glasgow University, who, with his fifteen native assistants, is pushing the work up into Eastern, Central and Western Sikkim, building their little churches almost on the borders of the perpetual snows; for in Sikkim rise those giant mountains 23,000, 25,000 and 27,000 feet high, towered over by their monarch Kinchin Janga, The Golden Horn, 28,177 feet high, the second highest mountain in the world.

With a hearty vote of thanks to the chairman, the speakers, and to Sir Charles and Lady Elliott, and a cheering cup of coffee as we passed out through the refreshment room again, we separated, with the intensified conviction and determination that "from the eternal snows of the Himâlayas to the scorching sands of Cape Comorin Jesus shall be King."

XXVII

THE ORIENTAL "BRIDE OF THE LAMB"[1]

I AM asked as to the "Cost of Foreign Missions." Is it not a very expensive agency? Does it produce adequate results? This is a fair question if asked in a proper spirit, with a desire to remedy defects and help forward the work.

I have prepared and brought here statistics with reference to your foreign missionary work which prove that it is one of the most economical agencies ever utilised by the Reformed Church for the establishment of churches and the bringing in of souls into the Kingdom, and the education and elevation of a people: but the lateness of the hour forbids my presenting these statistics now.

Yet, for the moment, grant that the missionary work does cost, and that it costs heavily. What then?

Mr. President, Brothers, Sisters: This is prob-

[1] The concluding part of an address before the General Synod of the Reformed Church, on Foreign Missionary Evening, at Catskill, N. Y., June 8th, 1896.

ably the last time that I shall ever be permitted to address the General Synod of the Reformed Church. Thirty-seven years ago this month I attended the meeting of the General Synod in Albany, then ordained and under appointment to sail to join the Arcot Mission. Twice before during this thirty-seven years I have returned, broken down, to my native land for recuperation, and have had the opportunity to plead with you for India, ere rejoining my field. Now, a third time God has heard prayer and granted such restoration that I look forward with joy to a speedy return to my chosen life work.

Fifteen years' work, in completing the translation and revision of the Telugu Bible, and in the bringing out of an illustrated Bible Dictionary written from an Oriental standpoint for Oriental people, for which I have been for twenty years preparing, and other literary and missionary labour has been laid on my shoulders, and how am I straitened until it be accomplished. My heart is pulling at the leash to get back this fall and throw my every energy into the work.

At my age, and in India's treacherous climate, there is little human probability that I shall again see the land of my birth. Nor would I have it otherwise. It is my earnest prayer that I may be summoned up with the harness on; that my body may be laid in the cemetery there among my people; and that, when the trump shall sound, I may go up surrounded by my spiritual children whom God has allowed me to bring out of heathenism's darkness into His light.

I desire then, in this probably my last address to you, to say a few very earnest words.

Grant that the missionary work does cost. What then? Nature teaches us that the higher the order of being, the longer the period, and, the more expensive the process of development. The inhabitants of a cube of moist cheese are born, developed and complete their life work in a few hours. The lamb gives a fleece at the end of the first year that pays all the expense of its rearing. The blooded colt requires three or four or more years of care and costly nurture before it brings any return to its owner.

The daughter of parents of culture; how carefully is she nurtured that her physical, intellectual and spiritual powers may attain the most perfect development. No expense is spared for doctors, teachers, advisers, as she goes on through primary, grammar and high school, and on to Wellesley, or Barnard. For two and a half decades the parents' care, the parents' wealth is lavished upon her that she may become an ornament to society, an uplifting agency in the world.

Brothers and sisters of the Reformed Church, you are nurturing a "Bride for the Lamb" in India, in China, in Japan, in Arabia. On you devolves the joyful task that she should be fitly cultured to be "The Lamb's Wife" to eternity. Who, who would complain of the expense needed for the proper culturing of these Oriental Brides of Christ? The Reformed Church aims to present to her Lord, as His bride, "The king's daughter all glorious within," adorned with pearls not bought in the market, pearls of character, pearls of devotion, pearls of absolute consecration to her Lord. "So shall the King greatly desire her beauty." Who would complain if she does not reach her maturity in one decade or two; if she requires many long years, as we measure years, for her growth, her culture, her adornment!

O, Church of the Redeemed! begrudge no care, no labour: Be not a stingy mother, nor impatient, for she whom thou dost nourish in those far lands of the Orient is for all ages to be "The Wife of the Lamb."

Four and a half decades ago I heard and heeded a summons to become a tutor to that bride in

India, a summons that after all these intervening years, and with my maturer powers, still rings, and with tenfold force, in my listening ears:

> "My soul is not at rest; there comes a strange
> And secret whisper to my spirit like a dream of night,
> That tells me I am on enchanted ground:
> The voice of my departed Lord, 'Go teach all nations,'
> Comes on the night air, and awakes mine ear.
> Why stay I here? The vows of God are on me,
> And I may not stop to play with shadows,
> Or pluck earthly flowers, till I my work have done,
> And rendered up account. . . .
> It matters not if storm or sunshine be
> My earthly lot; bitter or sweet my cup.
> I only pray, 'God fit me for the work,
> God make me holy and my spirit nerve
> For the stern hour of strife.' Let me but know
> There is a watchful eye that plans my path,
> An arm unseen that ever holds me up,
> And I will joy to tread the darksome wilderness.
> And when I come to stretch me for the last
> Beneath the Cocoa's shade, it will be sweet
> That I have toiled for other worlds than this:
> And through the ages of eternal years
> My spirit never shall repent
> That toil, and hardness once were mine below."

This is the inspiration with which I hasten back to India; my India, nay, nay, *Christ's India*, revolted indeed, but a part of which you and I, we of the Reformed Church, have sworn to bring back to its allegiance to our Lord.

May this be the aspiration, the inspiration,

with which we each spring forward to the work to which our Master summons us, while we hear before us His inspiriting voice, "Be thou faithful unto death, and I will give thee the Crown of Life."